Big Club,
Small Town
& Me

Published in the United Kingdom by TH Media in Derbyshire

ISBN 978 – 0 – 9559534 – 1 -5

First published in paperback in 2009

British Library Cataloguing in Publication Data:
A catalogue record for this book is available from the British Library.

Design and Marketing by Llama PR in Manchester

Printed by Digital Book Print Limited in Milton Keynes

Pictures reproduced by kind permission of Burnley Football Club

CONTENTS

My thanks go to my wife, Ellen, for all her wonderful support through the past few years, to my senior colleagues at Modus who have worked so hard during such challenging times, to my eldest brother Steve for his friendship and advice in producing this book, and to my late mother Teresa and my father Duncan to whom I owe so much.

Foreword by Tony Livesey

Well, it had to happen I suppose.
I should have known.
If I failed to make £100m and live out my dream for long enough, some jammy so and so would get in first and do it for me.
That so and so is Brendan Flood.
Talk about fantasy football!
Brendan must be the envy of every Burnley fan alive.
Self-made man, personal shopper on tap at C & A, King of Rawtenstall and now holder of a season ticket for life in those posh white bucket seats in the Bob Lord stand for the use of which we'd all trade our children.
(Or is that just me?)
Best of all, Brendan has enjoyed a bird's-eye-view of a season that has surely been the most remarkable ever seen at historic Turf Moor.
Along with chairman Barry Kilby, Brendan has helped to steer the Clarets to the promised land of the Premier League after 33 years in the wilderness.
(And no, I don't mean Rawtenstall).
What a year!
We've all seen the games, we've all marvelled at Owen Coyle's knee-length socks, we've all cried against Spurs, we've all ducked as the Red Devil hit the roof, we've all laughed at Bikey wrestling to remove his vest, we've all covered our wife's eyes as Robbie showed his underpants, we've all been to Wembley.
But....

That's where OUR story ends and Brendan's begins.

With this book he takes us behind the scenes at the Turf to an unseen world of tearful heart-to-hearts with doomed managers, nail-biting transfer deals, threats of financial meltdown and critical negotiations over the meat and potato pie contract.

There's not much advice a multi-millionaire can ever take from a bloke who makes a living reading the sports news on the telly but apparently the fact you are now privy to all these things is down to me.

I interviewed Brendan for the BBC when he first became involved with the Clarets.

I was full of sage advice.

Always leave your seat 20 minutes before half-time if you want to try to order a pint.

Never be tempted to wear the complimentary boardroom tartan rug over your knees - or if you do wear it short so the Longside think it's a kilt.

And never run naked past Bertie Bee.

Plus... I advised him to keep a diary.

And here it is.

Not many of us will ever be Barry or Brendan in real life so take this unique chance of a 'virtual' seat in the Burnley Boardroom.

Free tartan rug with every copy.

Well, not really.

That was one of my ideas he managed to ignore.

Up The Clarets
Tony Livesey
BBC Presenter

1

In For a Penny ...

4th December 2006

"There's no such thing as a free lunch." Anon

If you've picked up this book it's probably because you want to share in one of the most romantic football stories in recent times. As a long serving fan on the terraces my dream for the past 33 years has been to see Burnley in the Premier League. After all, when I was baptised as a Claret in 1967 we were beginning our gradual descent towards the bottom of the old fourth division.

The incessant struggle was defined by the emotional victory over Orient in 1987 which avoided the awful possibility of a lifetime of amateur football at Turf Moor. The evolution of cash fuelled super clubs with Sky TV marketing and global billionaire owners has, during the last twenty years, made the Premiership dream less likely. Burnley is a small town with a locally owned football club and local fans. The fifties and sixties bestowed upon us a portfolio of wonderful memories and a supporter network which extends way beyond the

Lancashire hills. Only a special mix of people, a bit more cash and a sprinkling of good luck would give us a chance of ending the struggle.

By sharing my experiences from November 2006 until now I want to make a statement for the club to celebrate its traditions and show that real football clubs, with predominantly British players, still have a major part to play in the modern Premiership. Burnley's youth tradition in the sixties saw a conveyor belt of talent emerge and once again, the club will seek out young, hungry players who want to play in the world's greatest league.

Since 2003 we have all experienced the most extraordinary boom and bust economy since the 1930s. Having established my business, Modus, in the heart of the 1991 recession I had always operated a cautious approach to investing beyond my core business. The boom encouraged me to diversify and to build up a nationally recognised group. Over the last three years I have suffered a frightening change in fortunes which have produced a complete juxtaposition to the emotional highs at Burnley football Club. Escaping the global downturn was like running away from a Tsunami – but at least I'm alive to tell the story.

◆

For my part, I just want to do the very best that I'm capable of and that's about it. It doesn't matter whether I'm working in my business or helping to drive our beloved Burnley Football Club on to greater glory I will always graft to achieve a degree of success. In essence, you get what you give in life.

So how did I come to invest in a football club? For that matter why does anybody invest in a football club? In many cases there is undeniably an element of status seeking that convinces successful businessmen to part with their hard earned cash. And in the days when that meant a few grand offered up by a local business leader then status was often the highest incentive.

Since then football has altered beyond all recognition. And now people and corporate players are investing for all kinds of reasons. It is extremely unlikely that a football club will hold the majority of an investor's attention. After all, most directors have a day job too. Nevertheless there are some powerful motives that drive people to invest. And at one end of the scale there are those who have a pure and unquestioning love. Anyone who meanly poured scorn on Delia Smith's half time rallying call at Carrow Road a couple of years ago missed the point. Yes of course it was funny. But right there in the centre circle on a windswept Norfolk night was a statement of love for the community and town that demonstrated her raw passion and commitment.

And believe it or not, sometimes the motive is money. The waves of American, Russian and Middle Eastern cash washing through the Premiership has changed the face of our game forever. To some wealthy individuals maybe a football club is little more than an expensive toy. But others, perhaps those with a bit less liquidity, can see the potential return of a truly global brand.

So where do I sit on this scale that is weighed down on one side by eccentric fans with a bit of spare cash and on the other by merciless businessmen and their army of accountants?

It's really not that simple.

When I made my way into the Chairman's Lounge for my first board meeting at Burnley Football Club, a long two and a half years ago, I did for a moment wonder how I'd got there. What had prompted me to put a £500,000 investment into the club to secure my place on the board?

I had never been in the Chairman's Lounge at Turf Moor before but I was immediately struck by an overwhelming sense of longevity. The whole room, with its oak panelled walls, and distinctive bar in the corner was steeped in history. It was clear from everything I saw that the club had existed forever. And it seemed to me that the character of the room was unchanged since the club's beginning in 1882. That is apart from the ridiculous stuffed cat that sits on a windowsill. The cat has sat there for years as part of a bizarre tradition between Burnley and Gillingham Football Club. Apparently it brings us good luck and Gillingham bad luck. Football fans being what they are in terms of logic, commonsense and perspective, it's obviously never going to move.

Long before the cat had become an attractive haven for insects, this lounge had seen chairmen, directors and managers planning and arguing long into the night in their shared quest to see Burnley succeed or, at times, just survive.

The bar had dispensed the right drinks at the right time to fuel celebrations of League Championships, FA Cup triumphs and countless wonderful victories. I'm sure it had also helped to dull the pain of defeat and the anxiety that was so prevalent throughout the eighties.

The boardroom is the Chairman's Lounge and, in keeping with the unplanned austerity, is adorned by pictures of Turf Moor from the early nineteen hundreds and framed shirts of historic legends. The overall sensation is one of an establishment with a rich heritage and most poignantly, misty eyed views of glory days gone by.

I imagined the redoubtable Bob Lord, arguably the most famous of all the Burnley Chairmen, who was incumbent at the club when I was a small lad, in his pin striped suit bossing the manager and players around. I wondered about the endless transfer negotiations that must have taken place in this room. How were the deals to move away heroes like Jimmy McIlroy, Ralph Coates and Martin Dobson, some of the greatest Clarets of all time, thrashed out? I could almost see Bob Lord shouting his defiance as the rest of the board took cover.

But this was 2006 and, as I took my place at the table, as one of the club's ten directors, I knew that I had taken on a huge responsibility as a custodian of the club that means so much to so many people. Family, school friends and business associates have peppered my daily conversation with intrigue and excitement from the events emanating from this very room, the heart of the club. But as the chairman, Barry Kilby, opened the meeting I found myself wistfully running through my mind a kaleidoscope of my world and what might have happened at the very table where I now sat - just as any fan would. And soon the earliest memories of my association with the Clarets came flooding back.

♦

I was the fifth of six children, three girls and three boys. Mum had the measure of all of us just like most mums bringing up their broods in Rawtenstall in the nineteen sixties. And she relied on Dad's backing in her ongoing battle to keep us all in order and the house in one piece.

Saturdays were Mum's respite days and her mantra to Dad was, 'just get the kids out of the house'. And whether I liked it or not, for me that meant going down the Turf with my dad and brothers, Steve and Chris. On the day of my first experience of football I didn't really want to go. Not out of any positive dislike, more out of ambivalence. I didn't understand the attraction because there had been nothing to capture my imagination. There wasn't much football on television so, like all young lads at that time, going to the match was a case of stepping into the unknown.

So on Saturday October 11th in 1969, at the raw age of seven, I boldly went where I hadn't been before. And determined to pass the time I went armed with a handful of my best conkers. Imagine trying to get into any football ground with such offensive weapons nowadays!

Burnley were playing Crystal Palace in a Division One fixture, and while I didn't really understand what was going on, I was struck by the sheer number of people at the match It was like church times five hundred! We stood at the back of the Longside terrace near the corner that met the open Bee Hole End. Even though I was one of the shortest in a crowd of over 12,000 I could still see the action on the muddy surface below. Turf Moor in the sixties was a bog and I was intrigued to see how far the players could run without the ball sticking in the mud.

Not that I watched much of the game. I attached one of my conkers to the crash barrier that Dad was leaning against and started playing.

We were 2-1 down at half time and the forty five minutes had passed for me without event. But in the second half I noticed a big difference. I can remember there was an awful lot of noise and everyone around me were getting more and more excited. This captured me and I became drawn into the atmosphere. Eventually Burnley won 4-2 and I had become caught up in the fervour of the crowd by mimicking the goal celebrations which were awesome.

It had been a good day and I had become a Claret.

A couple of Saturdays later, as Mum signalled that our presence in the house was no longer required, I was already excited at the prospect of another visit to Turf Moor with Dad and my brothers . There was no stepping into the unknown for me now. I knew what to expect and I couldn't wait to be among the crowd and hear the songs and observe the swear words and humour. I had started a habit that was going to last a lifetime. One that would cost me unimaginable amounts of cash, cause me to shed endless tears, feel utter despair, indescribable joy and intense pride.

Sheffield Wednesday was the opposition and Burnley won 4-2 again. So this was how I thought it would always be - an afternoon of assured delight punctuated by moments of near explosive ecstasy. I can think of a few hundred occasions since when a visit to the Turf could be more accurately described as torture; but at that time it seemed to me that winning was our right.

And the atmosphere was intoxicating, literally. We celebrated goal after goal amidst a thick cloud of tobacco and beer splashes, as the fans at the back of the Longside sang a whole repertoire of songs.

Understanding the words wasn't always easy for a seven year old but they did help to develop my knowledge of different parts of the country. When the Clarets played Liverpool I was a bit disturbed to hear the fans sing:

"In their Liverpool slums...
They look in the dustbin for something to eat,
They find a dead cat and they think it's a treat...."

I pondered this for a while and then I asked Steve, 'Do they really eat cats in Liverpool?' I had no idea where Liverpool was but I had started to form an idea about other places in the country, albeit exaggerated and often distorted. The chant:

"We hate Nottingham Forest, Liverpool and Man United," helped me to understand the tribalism that dominates football.

Being a football fan was very much like going on a cultural geography trip!

So a lot of my earliest memories were of the songs on the terraces, but something on the pitch also caught my eye. It seemed to me that the most exciting and involved of all the players in Claret and Blue were the wingers and that says a lot about the style of football we played forty years ago. That has always stayed with me. I've always loved watching a team with quick and skilful wingers plying their trade; and now the younger Burnley fans have felt the same exhilaration watching Wade Elliott's and Chris Eagles' electrifying displays this year.

Back then there were no lime green boots and gel spiked hair but the players were still brilliant and glamorous. On one wing Ralph Coates terrorised full backs with his trickery and combed over locks that inspired a generation of lookalikes, notably Sir Bobby Charlton and the Scottish comedian Gregor Fisher.

On the other flank was the young Steve Kindon, or 'Skippy' as he was known. He earned the nickname by developing an ungainly bounding style of running that was faster than anything any Burnley fan had seen. Whenever Coates or Skippy received the ball you could hear the buzz of excitement spreading around the ground. And it invariably ended with Frank Casper busting the net to the sound of the explosive roar that would have made the hair stand up on the back of my neck.

Being a Burnley fan in those days was like religion. You were born into it. I was starting to understand the game and the relationship that the team had with all of us on the terraces. We were like one big, chanting, happy congregation. But it wasn't long before I was brought crashing back down to earth at the end of the 1970-71 season.

I thought that I had joined a club where everyone, the players and the supporters, would stay for the whole of their lifetime, just like any family. I understood that the players would stop playing when they got older (not that Graham Alexander has realised that yet) but I assumed they would then become fans and join us on the terraces.

I understood when Dad had told me that we had been relegated to the second division. I guess that pain didn't hit me as hard as my older brothers because I knew that the football would carry on, and winning would be as much fun as it had always been. But five days after the season had finished something unimaginable happened that broke my heart, opened my eyes and awakened a whole new realisation in me.

The newspaper dropped though the letterbox of our Rawtenstall home and, after Dad had absorbed the bones of the reports, I saw the headline on the back page. I felt like I'd been hit in the face by Mum's biggest frying pan:

'Burnley Sell Coates'

I couldn't believe my eyes. Ralph Coates was my favourite player, my idol. How on earth could this have happened? Coates was part of our family and now, apparently, some one at the club had sold him!

In near panic I asked Dad what had happened. It turned out that Arsenal had made a bid for my favourite player as soon as the season was over. But it was Spurs who had bought him for a British record transfer fee of £190,000. It was all over the back pages of every national newspaper in the land, and on the front page of the Burnley Express. I still couldn't understand it. Surely we didn't just sell our best players. How and why could that happen?

Dad explained to me that there were decisions made at the club by Bob Lord who was the chairman. As tears filled my eyes he helped me to understand that this Bob Lord, a local butcher of legendary status, owned the club. And he decided who should stay and who should go.

While it seemed to me that selling Ralph Coates was the most stupid decision anyone at the club could have made, at the same time I was being educated that there was some all powerful boss-man who controlled everything that was happening on and off the pitch. As a nine year old I imagined he was one step down from Harold Wilson. You never see him but he's directing everything that happens in the world of our football club.

This experience had created a kind of mystique for me; I started to wonder what it was that made the club do certain things. So from a very early age, from the moment that Ralph Coates had been sold, I was intrigued by who it was that made the moves to decide the team and the club's future.

♦

For any Burnley fan of a certain age the spectacular seventies will always stick in your mind. This was a period in time which was epitomized by the conflicting emotions of joy and fear. We had the endless joy of watching the Claret kings, Waldron, Dobson, Fletcher, Casper, Noble and James filling us with pride week after week. And then we had the constant fear of having our heads kicked in by rampaging fans.

I think it was on Boxing Day in 1973 that I first learnt the meaning of true fear at a football match. Students of the heritage of football songs will tell you that this was the occasion that spawned the chant:

"Hark now hear the Burnley sing, the Geordies ran away,

And we will fight for ever more, because of Boxing Day."

With the benefit of a safe distance of hindsight football fans often tend to have a healthy dollop of bravado. But this was not exactly how I remember it. The only things that I can accurately recall were that Tommy Cassidy, who later came to play for Burnley, was playing that day for Newcastle, and that there were a lot of chants of:

"A – G, A – G – R, A – G – R –O, AGRO!"

Catchy. For all I knew the Geordies ate people, never mind cats. And we didn't hang around to find out. But I further developed my cultural knowledge of songs related to geography as this was the first time that I heard the Geordies sing 'The Blaydon Races', which our Longside lyricists soon adapted to 'The Burnley Aces'.

There must be some truth in the historical notion that the further north you go the more frightening the natives become. Both the Normans and the Romans struggled to subdue the North.

When Celtic visited East Lancashire for the euphemistically named Anglo Scottish Cup (The Culloden Shield would have been nearer the mark) everyone in Burnley pretended to speak with Scottish accents all day. We were all ready for the menacing tap on the shoulder from a Celt asking, 'hwit teym is it paaal?', knowing full well that any phonetic frailty would likely result in the receipt of a can of Tenants in your face.

But with most of the population of Burnley sounding like Fife Robertson for the day, the match passed with relatively little incident. We won 1-0, dodged a hail of urine filled bottles and went home. The Burnley Express carried a front page picture of a young lad with a dart stuck in his forehead. It didn't occur to me at the time but I now wonder how, in the nineteen seventies before the age of digital technology and mobile phones, they got this picture. I'm not for a minute suggesting that Peter Higgs, the sports editor, persuaded the lad to let him shove the dart back into his head for the photo. So well done the Burnley Express!

By far the most terrifying experience I had watching Burnley came away at Bolton. I hadn't been to Bolton before and after my first experience thought very carefully before returning. But on this wet Wednesday night, as always, I set off with Dad and my mate Steve Tattersall in Dad's green Triumph full of hope and anticipation.

My memories of what happened between 7-30pm and 9-15pm have paled into insignificance as the events that unfolded after the match were certainly more exciting! When we returned to our car on the wasteland next to Burnden Park the old Triumph showed no sign of starting, much to Dad's frustration. Steve and I listened to the car spluttering and Dad cursing for a few minutes before we decided to set off to find a phone box to phone Steve's mum.

As any naïve and cocky supporters in a foreign land would, we were wearing our claret and blue scarves, a fact that didn't go unnoticed by a sizeable gang of Bolton fans. And clearly up for a bit of fun they chased us back down the road to our car. We were a good twenty yards ahead of them and had time to get into our paralysed transport and lock the doors.

Thankfully the car was fully brick-proof as the advancing mob hurled various bits of masonry at us out of the pitch black darkness. But then in a scene reminiscent of 'The Hills Have Eyes' the drooling mob of our crazed attackers started rocking the car. I was beginning to envisage having to chew on several pairs of Dr Martins when the most amazing thing happened.

Dad had seen enough. With an eerily steely determination, presumably modelled on Dirty Harry, he decided to get out of the car and single-handedly batter twenty Bolton fans. And to our eternal gratitude, surprise and mighty relief they all ran away into the darkness. Dad later admitted that he was scared stiff but he couldn't think of anything else to do. And I said to Steve:

"Soft gets them Bolton fans eh?"

But Dad was happy to take on the new mantle as our enforcer and saviour.

That era was all about joy and fear. It was enough to make me a fully paid up member of Burnley Football Club for life. Where else can you be so ecstatic and fear for your life at the same time?

As we neared the end of the decade the incidence of joy became rarer. Certainly the team of the seventies holds the greatest attachment for me. I will never forget Colin Waldron scoring the goal at Preston that took us back to the top flight in 1973. And the FA Cup semi-final in 1974 was an afternoon filled with pride, joy and sadness. For our younger fans at Burnley, the Carling Cup semi final against Spurs this year is the first occasion since then that can replicate that heady cocktail of emotions.

It was fantastic to be at Hillsborough on a fine spring day. We went full of belief that we could get to Wembley. Burnley were riding high in the First Division and we expected to win. The ground was packed to the rafters, one half a throng of the black and white of Newcastle and the other half a 25,000 strong sea of claret and blue. It was one of the biggest days of my young life.

To be honest, I couldn't see much of the game because we were right down at the front behind the goal. Watching twenty two blokes playing football at ground level through netting isn't easy. I'm told that we were playing all the football but that doesn't always get the right result on the day. And my delight turned to desolation in two brutal strokes.

As I said, my view wasn't the best but I couldn't miss Malcolm MacDonald charging at us with all the grace of a bow-legged bull, tossing aside our centre half Jim Thomson and then stretching the net with two crashing finishes. Not football in its purest form but SuperMac was certainly effective.

And that was that. The Geordie singing was the best I had ever heard as they boomed 'haway the lads' throughout the second half. It was a relentless mantra that lifted their team and seemed to hypnotise ours.

But nothing could soften the blow for me. Since the sale of Ralph Coates this was the toughest experience I'd had as a Burnley fan, but then again I was only thirteen, and there was always going to be much more to come!

As we tried to get out of the ground at the Leppings Lane End I remember being crushed against the barriers and I couldn't breathe. It was quite frightening. There was such a small gate for us to get through and the fact that all nine thousand moving towards the exit were trudging sadly was a blessing I suppose.

Fifteen years later, as we all watched the horrific events unfold in the very same end in the 1989 semi-final between Liverpool and Nottingham Forest, I remembered my own experience as clearly as if it had been that day. The evolution of seating and modernized stadiums couldn't come soon enough.

♦

After the end of the seventies every Burnley fan witnessed a sequence of downhill events. We watched in various states of bewilderment, disbelief, disgust and depression some of the worst football imaginable. And we seemed to lower our level at will. One of the biggest shocks of the seventies was when non-league Wimbledon beat First Division Burnley 1-0 at Turf Moor in the FA Cup. But less than a decade later we played them in the league as our downward path crossed their ascent.

There was no way out for the fans. I knew that I had to stay loyal. When times are bad the love dies, but the loyalty is like a religion. I think the fact that I was brought up as a roman catholic might have had something to do with my stoicism. I stayed as a Burnley fan I guess because I thought I had to.

It's not that I didn't have the chance to shake off the relationship with my childhood sweetheart, who in the seventies had been enthralling, glamorous and thrilling, who had now turned into a miserable, ugly hag! But I'm ashamed to say I did have a couple of brief flirtations when I went to work in London in 1984.

For a while I lived just around the corner from Loftus Road and so I went to watch Queens Park Rangers but that didn't work for me. I felt numb from the waist up all the way through the games. I did wonder whether all QPR fans felt like that but I guessed it was probably just me.

So I tried Arsenal. The football was better but equally boring and there was still no trace of an adrenalin rush when they scored. Perhaps that was because they always won 1-0. But more likely the way everything seemed to pass me by meant that I was still tied to my first love. I had to go back to the Turf and give it another try.

On some days the crowds were less than 2,000. And with genuine respect to the likes of Colchester and Barnet, it was desperately humiliating for anyone who had squeezed in to a jam packed Turf Moor only ten years earlier to see us beating Chelsea or Manchester United.

The feted Manchester City and Norwich manager John Bond had arrived in the early eighties, with his very big cigar, to save us from ourselves. His merry band of ageing, crocked and highly paid ex-City stars were still good enough to turn the club around, weren't they? Sadly for us, that wasn't the case. We soon found out that our vaunted internationals Tueart, Reeves, Gow, Donachie and, one of the first million pound signings, Steve Daly, weren't actually good enough to beat Halifax Town.

It just got worse and worse. And by the end of 1986 it had got as bad as it possibly could.

For some reason Boxing Day has often been an unhappy football day for the Clarets, but nothing can match Boxing Day in 1986 for unmistakably unadulterated misery. The Boxing Day fixture is a family tradition all over the country as fathers, sons, brothers and sisters shake off the excesses of Christmas Day with two pints, two pies and hopefully a win.

And this year was no different as we clapped the team out onto the pitch hoping for a bout of festive fun in a local derby with Rochdale. Sadly it turned out to be less fun than sticking pins in your eyes, as we witnessed ninety minutes of what you could loosely describe as football. It was simply dreadful. Our players were taking it in turns to fall over the ball or miss-kick it. We got two bookings and I can't for the life of me believe that either of the fouls was deliberate. It was utterly horrible. And predictably a 'workmanlike' Rochdale team ran out worthy 3-0 winners. I was horrified and bored with failure.

By the time we had lost our way through Easter it had dawned on even the most optimistic of Burnley fans that we were in danger. This was the first year that the league had decided to do away with the re-election formality and replace it with an automatic relegation for the bottom club. And on the eve of the last game of the season our decline had been so spectacular that things were out of our own hands.

The following day we were to play Orient, who were chasing a play-off place and had to win. But to retain our league status we had to rely on either Torquay or Lincoln to lose. Torquay were as bad if not worse than us so we just had to concentrate on our own game.

And what if we failed? It didn't bear thinking about. The team, my team, who had won the League, the FA Cup, played some of the best European teams and only eleven years ago had been in the top flight would be disappearing into the non-league abyss. To put it into context, a neighbouring semi-professional team, Colne Dynamoes, backed by a local businessman imaginatively named 'Chalky' White had a chance of being promoted to the league. The ignominy was indescribable.

Whether it was to come to the wake, or as I prefer to believe, be with the Clarets in their hour of need, 17,000 fans packed into Turf Moor on the 9th May 1987. I think that the sense of ultimate failure reignited a lot of fanaticism in Burnley fans and the atmosphere that day was emotionally charged to such a level that most of the 17,000 had shed a tear by the end of the day.

I went with an old mate of mine, Col Kennaugh, and we stood in our usual place on the Longside willing us on and subconsciously saying the Rosary over and over again. The whole place went crazy with relief when Neil Grewcock scored a sublime goal. And when Ian Britton, the shortest man on the pitch, if not in the ground, headed a second it felt like this was going to be our day.

When we held on to the final whistle the ground erupted and thousands of fans spilled onto the pitch. There are such fine margins between success and failure, but that day felt like success. We were saved.

But as I stood on the hallowed turf I didn't actually know whether we had survived. Apparently at Torquay a dog had run onto the pitch and bitten a linesman, probably not that unusual in Devon, but today of all days! The match down there had been delayed for fifteen minutes while they caught the dog and presumably tested the linesman for rabies. Only at Burnley could our agony be prolonged by a farce at the other end of the country in the land of Fawlty Towers.

At that very moment I experienced an altogether new combination of emotions, elation and fury. Being a Burnley fan will of course ultimately lead you to the madhouse. The pride in our club was at its highest, but within seconds the shame could quite possibly be at its deepest. How could it happen? How did we get into this awful mess? And what would Turf Moor become? A cattle market? A rugby ground? A ghost stadium? The unthinkable was being thought by everyone around me and human nature asked us where to lay the blame. Who had got us into this position, Bob Lord, John Bond or just a succession of poor players?

When the news came through that good old Lincoln had lost, the tears began to flow. Everybody felt it. Burnley has that real sense of togetherness when bad things are happening. We had escaped the worst of all nightmares and now we could all go home.

♦

It would never be so bad again. I bought a season ticket in the Bob Lord Stand and cheerily watched us as we steadily work our way upwards. The year after our near disaster and possible extinction 35,000 Burnley fans went to Wembley to see the green shoots of recovery in the Sherpa Van Final. We lost 2-0 to Wolves but in a way that didn't matter. We were still here. We were still a football club. We were starting to have fun again, and where better to start than Wembley?

Progress was steady after our near fatal shock and while there was a feeling of relief and euphoria in 1987 and 1988, it was always going to be a testing climb. For many years the lower league struggle was watched by small crowds of a few thousand and the relationship between players and fans naturally became closer as the players can hear everything that's said in the crowd.

During this lean period I went to a match at Bristol Rovers on a cold wintry night and unfortunately for the loyal band of Burnley fans there was no food kiosk open in our end of the ground. The Burnley substitutes were warming up in front of us halfway through the first half. One of our substitutes was Jamie Hoyland, a big, bruising midfielder with an uncompromising attitude. A fan in front of me leant over onto the pitch and shouted:

"Jamie, come over here!"

Jamie trotted over, probably expecting an autograph request but not so:

"Jamie, there's no grub in here and we're starving. Can you run up their end and get us a pie and peas and a Bovril?"

"Give us a fiver then," Jamie replied and off he went up to the other end of the pitch where a Bristol fan duly obliged. Within five minutes Jamie had delivered the order. How's that for service with a smile!

We won promotion in 1992, and then again in 1994 to what was, at that time, the First Division (Second Division to the traditionalists). That turned out to be a step too far too early and we were relegated the following year. But as time progressed I started to wonder whether at some stage I might get involved myself. I had always enjoyed being associated with the club as a fan. I'd been through thick and thin for a quarter of a century. From the very first understanding I had of the deal that took Ralph Coates away, I still held a fascination for what went on at the club off the pitch. As a fan you always assume it's beyond you and I was no different. It's difficult to imagine yourself owning a football club.

I knew that a lot of the reasons for the club's failure in the eighties went a lot deeper than just mediocre ability with a football. And maybe there would be an opportunity for me to try my own hand at some point in the future. By the late nineties my business was maturing and I was getting myself into a position financially where I could have joined the board. Barry Kilby had taken over at the club and was ready and clearly able to take it to the next level. The directors knew that I potentially had the financial clout to help the club. But I didn't think that I could have made enough of a difference at the time. And in any case, I was focussed on my business. At the time I didn't think I had the energy or the capacity to make a real difference at Burnley.

I had observed that in the seventies and eighties football clubs were run by butchers and bakers, like Bob Lord and Martin Edwards at Manchester United, but by the nineties they were owned by millionaires. With the advent of Sky the Premiership soon became the domain of multi-millionaires and now it is the billionaires' province. These days it's in the Championship where you find the multi-millionaires and so the landscape has changed for anyone who wants to be part of a football club. It's competitive on and off the pitch. The business model is unusual because most clubs now generate media based revenues, so owners and managers need accomplished commercial and PR skills.

In financial terms there is a huge difference now between the Championship and League One. In the Championship you need to have Premiership capability in terms of finance, stadium and infrastructure. You have to have the ambition to take that final step because if you try to tread water there's a fair chance you'll sink.

And for my part, I always need to know that I am making a positive impact. So I watched from my seat in the Bob Lord Stand, as Barry Kilby became chairman with Stan Ternent as manager and took the Clarets into a bright new era in the twenty first century. Under Stan things were always happening and after he secured promotion back to the second tier we even had two flirtations with the play-offs at the beginning of the decade. Stan was Burnley personified; tough, determined and uncompromising and he had helped to firmly re-establish the club in the Championship. But then a couple of years later Stan ran out of steam and parted company with the club, to be replaced by Steve Cotterill.

A lot of my upbringing was about working in a team from the very early years, as one of six children. I had grown my business in that way and by 2006 I believed that I was in a good position to contribute some new ideas to the club.

The first time I thought about making the step forward was at a home match against Birmingham City late in November. Our opponents were leading the league and were strong favourites to go up. But we were having a good season too and sitting in fourth place. We lost 2-1 to a late deflected goal, but I thought that we had played well and we looked capable of beating them. It seemed to me that we could live with the best team in the division and maybe it just needed a little bit more finance.

Barry and his vice chairman Ray Ingleby had called to see me a couple of times in 2005. But I wasn't overly keen to join the board then because I didn't think that I could give the time and I was unsure about the financial commitment generally.

I had got to know Ray as we used the same lawyers and he soon started to canvass me from time to time. I like Ray. He's an out and out salesman, like Gordon Gecko in his approach. He's very quick to see the upside in a deal, a real entrepreneur.

Ray was attracted to Burnley by the potential for it to become a media proposition as the media sector is his background. And at the time when ITV Digital was throwing money at the Championship he could see the possibilities. But the subsequent collapse of ITV Digital made the pot of gold at the end of Ray's rainbow vanish into thin air. Thereafter he knew that the club would have to be run on business fundamentals, and someone else needed to shoulder the drive forward.

Barry was keen to find help as well. He had become a bit battered and bruised by his period in charge. He had taken most of the responsibility for managing the money on a day-by-day basis. And he had invested up to four and a half million pounds of his own money, by far the biggest commitment in the club's history at that time. Barry is one hundred per cent committed to the club doing well. But he was clearly feeling weary after the demise of ITV Digital, and how it had nearly pushed the club into administration.

So a week after the Birmingham game I shook hands with Barry and that was it. After years of wondering just how the powerful Churchillian figure in the boardroom pulled everybody's strings I was about to find out. I have to admit that at the time I agreed to join the club I wasn't fully informed of the board's intentions until I was actually sat in there.

That week I went to the club's AGM armed with my cheque. The nine incumbent directors all sat at the front and I sat at the back as a director in waiting. A special resolution had been passed to increase the size of the board to ten so I was ready to go. Rather naively I thought that my appointment might be high on the agenda but it turned out that the principal question on the night was the change of the pie contract!

Dave Edmondson, the chief executive, had to field an avalanche of questions from shareholders as to why we had changed to Hollands from a local supplier. I stared in wonder as the debate raged on passionately. Why were we withdrawing our support from a local supplier? We shouldn't necessarily change for the benefit of sponsorship and, after all, we had come third in the Four Four Two 1998 second division pie league. I won't go as far as saying that I was wavering at that point but it was certainly very interesting. This was my first experience behind the scenes at the club and clearly there was much to think about as a director.

At the end of the great pie debate I went to chat to Barry and he introduced me to Steve Cotterill. I was intrigued to meet Steve and to see what he was like one-to-one. We talked about the club and where I had come from, and I gave him my card and asked him to call me at any time to talk about his vision for the club. I think Steve detected a new kind of interest in the board and it wasn't long before he contacted me.

I gave Barry my cheque for £500,000 and agreed to attend the board meeting the following week. Apart from the fact that you can never take the question of pies too lightly, I had already learnt something else about the way the club was run. Half a million bought me a seat on the board and all that comes with it. Sitting in the comfy white seats on the half way line, enjoying the five star food, a car park pass outside the front door and a ticket to the chairman's lounge at every away match. You can then be a director as long as you want and you're not obliged to contribute new cash ever again. That was standard procedure at Burnley. But it seemed to me that the club was in danger of lagging behind the others in our league and we had a late eighties feel to our business. Anyhow, I was here now, so I decided to see how I could help.

I had told my wife, Ellen, that I was investing in the football club. It wasn't such a big deal at that time, Ellen knows how much the football club means to me and she was happy for me. But it wasn't long before I was going to test Ellen's impressive level of tolerance.

◆

So there I was, sitting in the boardroom at my first meeting with the directors of our proud football club Burnley. The same Burnley that had taken me to the heights of ecstasy, and then to the depths of miserable despair. I knew nothing of the stuffed cat before but I knew all about Coates, Waldron, Fletcher, Grewcock, Liverpudlian eating habits and Bolton fans' hobbies and I know what Glaswegian urine smells like and I can instantly imagine that indescribable joy that everyone feels when the ball hits the back of the net and the Clarets roar.

After what must have been fifteen minutes of sentimentality fuelled day-dreaming my attention very suddenly clicked back to the room. Barry had started to talk about the club's wage bill. The players wages were running at four and a half million, which in Steve Cotterill's estimation was too low to sustain a team in the Championship. And he was probably right. In football you get what you pay for, more often than not.

But to my utter amazement the consensus among the directors was that we'd have to get the wage bill down to two and a half million by the end of the season! I thought my quarter of an hour of day-dreaming must have addled my brain. Maybe I was still dreaming. Sadly not, and as someone who had just handed over a cheque (which presumably had already been banked) I was trying to take it all in.

While the sombre mumblings went on I quickly worked out that we had a competitive side but we were in danger of getting out of our depth after Christmas. Our star striker, Andy Gray, had got injured against Leeds, in time honoured fashion, and we needed a replacement. Steve knew he needed to bolster the squad. But here and now the directors were talking about reducing the wage bill to two and a half million. I was horrified.

I had obviously pitched in at a very bad time, which wasn't absolutely clear to me at the point when I handed my cheque over. The reality of my situation was becoming rapidly and alarmingly obvious to me. I thought 'we're going to go down here. I've just paid half a million quid and we're bloody well going to go down.' I could have just kept my seat in the Bob Lord Stand and saved myself the worry.

To my abject horror everyone around the room seemed to be in agreement. I hadn't intended to shout up too much in my first meeting but I couldn't stay quiet any longer:

"Excuse me Gentlemen. I've just put half a million pounds in because I thought we were going to push up the league, and not vote for mediocrity."

The mood of the meeting was really sombre as we continued to discuss the proposed wage cuts. As a fan, I couldn't face the prospect of relegation.

I looked around the hushed room with a measure of disbelief, I made what can only be described as a quick decision, almost an impulse. To be honest I couldn't think what else to do so I put my cards on the table:

"Okay I'll tell you what I'll do. I'll put in another two million during next week and we'll go the other way."

As I said that I could almost sense eight of the directors diving off their chairs and hiding under the table. They were all wondering what had happened and they shared a palpable disbelief that I had been so forthright about my commitment.

But I simply wasn't prepared to associate myself with the club in an environment where we were preparing to fail. The only reason I joined the board was to help build success, not failure. If there wasn't even a chance of winning then I didn't want to be around.

You could have heard one of the fleas on the stuffed cat have a heart attack as we were consumed by an uneasy silence for a good ten seconds. Then Chris

Duckworth, who has been an enormous Burnley fan all his life, plonked his pen down on the table and said:

"Fantastic! Get in! That's what we need!"

Chris is a lovely bloke, he has plenty of jokes about him and he's completely committed to the club. He'd joined the board after he built up his company TeleCity to an impressive value in the late nineties. And Chris is passionate about the club and so he was magnificently vocal in his support.

So at that very moment, indirectly and in a moment of impulse, I had inadvertently stepped further forward than I had ever planned to at Burnley Football Club. I was determined to see this proud club make a real challenge for promotion to the Premiership and return to the heights it had graced when I first sensed its magic almost forty years earlier. And I wasn't about to give anything less than my absolute best.

It was very clear to me from what took place at my first meeting that by joining the board I hadn't achieved a lifetime ambition, I had simply taken my place at the starting line.

2

What's So Hard About Banking?

1961 – 1988

*'Sometimes your best investments are the ones you don't
make.' Donald Trump*

Mum and Dad were both devout Catholics and they
brought us up with a clear sense of right and wrong. We
were never affluent but we had a secure and happy
upbringing. And while Dad always brought the money
home, it was Mum who was in charge of the house.

She pushed us all hard to achieve as well as we could
at school. She was immensely proud of us, but never let
us become complacent or proud of ourselves. Even at
primary school if I had come top of the class it was never
quite good enough for Mum. There was always some
way that I could have done better. And that set the
pattern. The target for me was always to do better than
my older brothers and sisters. There is an advantage to
being lower down in the family. You can watch and learn
from the mistakes that your older siblings have made.
But then you have to strive even harder because as you
try to achieve more than they have, you have less of an
excuse for failure. In some ways it was quite
unforgiving, but the lessons I learnt and the targets Mum

set have shaped the way I have done certain things in later life.

Mum had good reason to be proud. My eldest sister, Cath, who is five years older than me, was as near as you could get to the perfect daughter. She had a great singing voice, a lovely personality and was very generous. She did extremely well at school and was Head Girl at St Hilda's in Burnley. It was no surprise given her academic ability and kind nature that, after going to University, she became a teacher.

Colette was three years younger than Cath and as she was the nearest to me and we definitely suffered from sibling rivalry. We always have and we always will. Colette was a resolute character and she too was bright enough to become Deputy Head Girl at St Hilda's. You can see that we have a strong streak of responsibility in the family.

Nicola, the baby of the family, followed in her sisters' footsteps at St Hilda's before becoming a teacher too. All in all we were quite an academic family. Mum had never had the opportunity that we had and she was determined that we would all do well in life. She constantly chivvied us on in our school work because she believed that a university degree was essential to get a decent job. And she very nearly achieved her goal. All of her children went to university, except me.

While we were all academic, it's fair to say that two of us had a lot more fun on the sports field than in the classroom. Chris was completely sports mad. He was a very popular lad and he always had a joke in him. So I found it easy to like him too. He followed my eldest brother Steve to St Theodore's school in Burnley and was captain of the second eleven football team but his main sport was cricket and he soon became an accomplished cricketer.

After he left school Chris was in the Rawtenstall first team for a number of years. He was a useful spin bowler and famously took seven for forty in the 1976 Worsley

Cup final against Accrington. I think his collection is still a record for an amateur cricketer in the Lancashire League. There was a huge crowd there of over 4,000. And of course the Floods were all there to see Chris' triumph.

In fact it was a real family affair. I was doing the scoreboard, Dad was doing the scorebook and Chris was taking the wickets. It was a very memorable day for us all.

The family's passions were always football and cricket, either watching or playing, and when I was growing up Chris was the star. I spent a lot of time with him as a child and it became important for me to be good at sports because he was. Chris is still a Burnley fan but he has high standards and only likes to watch good football. So he's only just started coming back again this last year, since Owen Coyle became manager. I accuse him of being a part-timer but he's just honest. If the football isn't good he doesn't come to watch.

Between my eleventh and fifteenth years I went to school at St Mary's College in Blackburn and then a school in Newcastle for the fifth year as Dad moved jobs. But then we moved back to Lancashire and near Burnley.

So with an impressive family name to live up to at school I made my way to St Theodore's in the sixth form determined to be a success, particularly on the sports field. And eventually I was delighted when, at sixteen, I got a call up for the second eleven football team.

My debut was a home match against a local school in Preston. We always played our school matches on the football pitches at Townley Hall in Burnley. And I remember that this was a typically cold and wet November day. So, on an incredibly boggy pitch it was certainly not like watching Brazil.

I was playing at centre forward but as I waded about in six inches of mud I was finding it hard to get going. It didn't help that, being a year younger than most of the players, I didn't know the names of my team-mates. I spent a lot of the first half waving my arms and shouting for the ball in a desperate attempt to get into the game. But after a miserable forty-five minutes we went in 1-0 down.

The first few minutes of the second half were just as bad but then came the moment that will live in my rose tinted memory forever. After another of our hopeful punts forward, the Preston goalie collected the ball, and I made my way back to the half way line to turn and face. The goalie wandered to the edge of his box, wiped about half of the mud off the ball and then kicked it from his hand loosely in my direction.

And as the ball dropped it became evident that it was dropping to me. I had to decide in a split second whether to head it or kick it. So I just belted the ball, along with the mud still clinging to it, back from where it came.

It's better from here on if you try to imagine the action in slow motion.

The ball soared back towards the goalie and we all stared open mouthed, waiting to see what would happen. Ninety nine times out of a hundred the ball would have landed on the next pitch. But to mine and everyone else's utter amazement it flew over the stumbling goalie and into the net! And that legendary pre-Beckham moment was met by St Theodore's own style and wave of hysteria in the mud.

I think everybody thought, 'Bloody Hell what was that?' including our coach Mr Heap and I was immediately promoted to the senior first eleven team.

Suffice to say I never really quite reached those goal scoring heights again. I'm not saying that I was found out, but I did settle comfortably into my new role at centre half.

The year after I was made captain of the first team. The first eleven was a decent team at that time, and included David Miller who was the son of the Burnley manager Brian. We won the schools league and the following year formed our own club, Brunshaw Celtic, which we entered into the Burnley and Pendle Sunday League.

In the summers of my teenage years I played cricket for Rawtenstall until we moved over to Foulridge where I turned out for Barrowford and enjoyed the picturesque surroundings of the West Craven league. Life was mainly about football and cricket as a typical Lancastrian lad.

♦

I buckled down to my studies well enough to get good grades in my A-Levels, and they were acceptable enough to secure a place for me at Manchester University to study economics. I was looking forward to going and following in the footsteps of my older brothers and sisters. And Mum was pleased for me. She had pushed us all hard enough to get the results that she had hoped for. But shortly before I was due to go to Manchester the family had a change in circumstances that prompted me to reappraise my plans.

There had been problems brewing for a while at Coats Viyella, and so a lot of Dad's work had dried up and he was forced to look elsewhere. While it wasn't such a surprise, nevertheless it was bad news. Dad had done well throughout his career and had done a tremendous job in providing without fail for his big family. So this signalled the start of a worrying time for us all. And even though there was just me and Nicola still at home, this was unchartered territory.

There was less money coming in and Mum and Dad were starting to struggle financially. So I decided that the only thing to do was for me to get a job. In a way I was a bit gutted that I wasn't going to university but this seemed more important at the time. And I did have some fairly persuasive encouragement to follow this course of action from a good friend of mine. My old schoolmate, Colin Kennaugh, had left St Theodore's at sixteen and got a job at Barclays Bank in Burnley. It hadn't gone unnoticed to me that Col had managed to find himself a self sufficient lifestyle. He always had a few quid in his pocket, and not only did it seem like the bank had a lot of good looking girls, there was a great sports and social side to the job. It's hardly surprising that all of this quite appealed to me. And to be honest I wasn't particularly bothered what the work content was going to be, so long as the money was enough and the social side was good. So I went for an interview and landed a position in the tiny office of Barclays at the top of the hill in Colne.

I actually enjoyed my work at Barclays. At that time I had absolutely no ambition to move upwards in the bank but I worked hard and tried to please the boss. I did briefly have an ambition to become a sports journalist. I loved the idea of spending my time watching and writing about sport. So I enrolled myself on a typing course at Nelson and Colne College. I thought that if I was going to have any chance of being a sports journalist then at least I'd have to learn how to type.

So I registered at night school with dreams of writing football reports for the Burnley Express, to find that I was the only bloke among about twenty women, apparently aged between sixteen and sixty. We sat in four rows of desks, each with a typewriter. It was something of a surreal experience to be honest. In the context of the late nineteen seventies it was as if I had infiltrated a big typing pool and I shouldn't really have been there. From the furtive and suspicious glances I received from some of the older women in the class I got the impression that the ladies agreed. But the truth of the matter is that I was so bad at typing and so far behind everyone else in the room within ten minutes, that I think the tutor was quite pleased when I didn't return the next week.

So with that ambition quashed I was quite happy to just carry on at Barclays. But after a couple of years of this untroubled life the boss took it on himself to disturb my happiness and started to hint that I should be thinking about bettering myself. I knew that I was well regarded and he was aware that I'd achieved good results at school, so he probably knew better than me that I wasn't suited to working at Barclays in Colne for the next forty years.

I had been at the Colne branch for three years when an opportunity came up for me to go and work in London. I'd never been to London before but I had the chance to go on secondment with a two way ticket. And it was probably good timing for me. At the time I was playing football for St Theodores Old Boys on Saturdays and Brunshaw Celtic on Sundays. I was still enjoying my footy but Celtic had become a bit of a trophy hunting team. We'd had promotion after promotion and got into the top division. I was playing two matches at the weekend and training was twice a week. I loved playing the matches but didn't much like the training as I was doing night school classes for the banking exams at the same time. So I joined Barrowford Nomads for an easier life where the 'craic' was great and I made some friends that I still bump into at Turf Moor. Burnley F.C. and the local amateur teams are closely interwoven. You play football, you watch football and you talk football. That's how life is in the north and I knew that I'd miss it.

The secondment to London was for two years and at twenty-one it was just about the perfect time for me to go. I was scared but knew that I had to stretch myself beyond my comfort zone. At least I had a two year return ticket to the north and I always felt that I would come back one day.

♦

While I was in London the bank had organised for me to live in a big complex of student-style accommodation in Shepherds Bush. Could have been worse. The rooms were adequate if functional and mostly shared. I was rooming with a lad called Stuart from Middlesboro, who I soon nicknamed 'Stu the Perv'. He wasn't into football but he certainly had one hobby – porn!

When I arrived in the room I noticed he had two suitcases under his bed and thought he must have had a lot of clothes for a small bloke. Not so. Like most young men he actually had one pair of jeans, about five t-shirts and two pairs of underpants. But what he also had was two suitcases jam packed with porn magazines. His collection of jazz mags was so extensive that I think some of them were actually quite valuable. It's fair to say that Stu was a connoisseur of soft porn.

Happily there was a squad full of lads in the bank who could play football. There were single guys from all over the country working in London for the first time like me. So there was always the chance of a game of footy and the opportunity to get out of the flat. After a few weeks and in an attempt to give my weekends a bit more focus I decided to enter a team in the West London Sunday League. So we put a team together of all Barclays lads and our mates. I was given the responsibility of deciding what to call the team. So I tried to think of something different. I think the lads probably regretted trusting me to come up with a name when we were entered as Bayern North End (a clever, if unfathomable combination of Bayern Munich and Preston North End). But it was too late – I thought 'that'll do' and sent it in and BNE was born.

We had an excellent season in many ways. But I have to say it was largely shaped around a series of physical threats.

The Stamford Bridge Arms was, without doubt, the hardest team I ever played against. They made Vinny Jones and Chopper Harris look like a pair of Morris dancers. But being our first season in this league we didn't really know the form and after surviving ninety minutes of aggravated assault we limped off the field with a deserved, if painful, 2-0 victory.

The pitch we played on was an old recreation ground pitch and was very isolated. And as we left the changing rooms, battered and bruised and with an ill judged winning performance under our belts, it became clear that the nice boys from the Stamford Bridge Arms were waiting outside to give us another good kicking.

Faced with the distinct possibility of being on the end of a collective GBH my brave band of mates pushed me out of the door and said , 'go and sort it out Brendan'. So leaving my eleven pals in the sanctity of the dressing room I went outside and spoke to their captain. The best way I can describe him is he looked a bit like Ray Winstone would if you'd just run over his dog after visiting his missus. So I thought that an open approach would probably be the best and I said:

"Look mate, I know you're going to kick our heads in so, you know, why don't we just call it quits."

In all honesty I didn't think this strategy would be entirely successful but the response was a bit of a surprise. All of the Stamford Bridge team started flapping their arms and clucking like chickens. I don't think this was the first time they'd impersonated chickens and they carried on with some gusto as we casually walked past them and then legged it to the cars!

I'd like to say that this type of experience was untypical of most games in the West London League but it wasn't. Every Sunday it was a fair bet I was heading for a session of managed hooliganism interrupted only by the occasional trace of football.

Eventually the season came to a close and we were surprised when we received a summons to go to the league awards evening. We hadn't won the league but we had ended up a creditable half way and more surprisingly we were all still able to walk.

I wasn't sure what we had won, but I told the guys we'd been asked to go, so dutifully, on the night of the awards we all turned up. It was quite a big affair with five hundred people there and we had our own table somewhere near the back from where we watched the awards being handed out. We watched the League winner's award and then the runners up; then came the cup winners and the second division league winners. We started to think that we'd just been invited as a ruse to get the numbers up. But then the bloke with the microphone announced that we were coming to the 'special' awards:

"And the winner of the award for the Most Sporting Team in the whole league is ..... Bayern North End."

Cue less than rapturous applause and a wave of badly concealed sniggers. This was clearly in recognition of the fact that we were undeniably a team of pansies. But I like to think we played an attractive brand of football. We certainly improved our one touch style of play, although that was admittedly because nobody in our team wanted the ball!

And during the season two of my best pals, Steve Tattersall and Paul Nolan or 'Noddy' (on account of his big ears) also moved to London. It made the move to London great fun for the three of us.

♦

It was around this time, in my first year in London that I met my wife Ellen. It was at a party up in north London near Hornsey at a friend called Marion's house. Marion was a friend of Noddy's from Leicester Polytechnic. By this time I was having a memorable social life.

As we arrived at this particular do, my mate, Noddy said to me:

"Bren, keep you eyes open tonight, there's this lovely girl coming down from Manchester, she's a real beauty queen."

And he grinned at me with that deluded glint of confidence in his eye that only useless pissed blokes on the pull can have.

Ellen was a friend of Marion's from Chester Law School and was down visiting her for the weekend. She had qualified as a lawyer and was working up in Manchester doing her articles at Linder Myers. And to make extra money while she was training, Ellen entered beauty competitions. I was intrigued.

I made my way into the kitchen where Ellen was. And as an added bonus, as all young partygoers know, that's where the booze is, so there's always a fallback if plan A fails. But this time I certainly wasn't disappointed. Not only was Ellen lovely, but she seemed to like me! We were getting on really well and although she was in Manchester and I was in London we managed to keep in touch and got together as often as we could.

It turns out that Ellen was Miss Manchester City 1983. And that was her one and only experience of football before I met her.

♦

I was settling well into life down in London and was being promoted annually at work. But I was still very much the northern lad. In terms of banking you know who the bad guys are in Colne but London was an entirely different pool of piranhas all together. I have to admit that when I left the north I wasn't particularly streetwise. But if you have your head screwed on it doesn't take long to realise that there are some clever people in London who can take advantage of you.

It wasn't long before I was moved to the Barclays branch of Kingsland right in the heart of the East End. It was proper 'Eastender' territory, they had eel shops down the street which I'd previously thought were a feature of the eighteenth century. To actually see a shop that just sold eels was unbelievable to me. I wondered where the hell I had ended up.

Not long after I was put in charge of a local branch that was threatened with closure, Haggerston. It was just down the road from Kingsland and was best known for its array of gangsters that banked there. So not surprisingly this was a branch that the bank's inspectors looked at with serious misgivings albeit from a safe distance. They knew that most of the cash being paid in was unclean.

As soon as I arrived the officer who had been in charge of the branch gave me a list of names and said:

"Whatever you do Brendan, don't mess with these guys .Don't ask them for fire insurance, don't ask them to pay in and for Christ's sake don't charge them an arrangement fee. In fact don't do anything, otherwise you might see repercussions."

Now I'd dealt with difficult customers before and, displaying all my northern bravado, I laughed and said:

"What like?"

The officer looked at me and replied in a sort of resigned and matter of fact way:

"Well, the manager who was here three years ago was asked to come and clean it up and he started to agitate a few customers. So in his first week here he had his house professionally burgled. And after a month he had his car set on fire outside the branch."

I got the picture.

And as luck would have it, while I was in charge of the branch the Brinks Mat robbery happened. The following week, the police were in the branch going through all the money movements that had gone on in the past few days. Suffice to say that a lot of the money had already gone to Spain. And in all honesty, with my colleagues words ringing in my ears, every time we'd had an instruction to do an overseas transfer we just sent it!

For me being a country boy, this had been a real grown up experience of the world. During my spell in London I had learnt not to trust easily and that probably helped me enormously in terms of my business sense. You can get a good impression of someone the first time you meet and that's very important. But real trust is something that comes with time.

The two years training on the front line down in London had started to shape me as a businessman. I had a long way to go and an awful lot to learn. But it was a fantastic experience and one that I'll never forget.

And at the end of the two years I had the option to stay in London or go back home. Over the past few months I had been seeing more of Ellen and things were going well for us. So I decided to return north.

◆

When I arrived back in Lancashire I don't think Barclays knew what to do with me so I spent a few weeks in Blackburn, before being sent to run the branch at Stanley Street in Preston. It was a corner shop branch and a far cry from the East End of London. I think the nearest we came to a crime wave was when one of the pens on the counter snapped off its chain.

But it was so, so quiet. And to keep myself entertained during the day, I spent some of my time organising social trips for the staff in Preston. So I was delighted when I managed to get us booked on a trip to watch 'The Price is Right' being filmed live.

I'd organised a coach to take fifty of us to the show and we were all really excited. Slightly tongue in cheek I'd say to the girls in the branch:

"Hey when we go down to 'The Price is Right' what should I do when Leslie Crowther shouts, 'Brendan Flood come on down'? They're going to shout me because they always pick the leader because they're the popular ones aren't they? Shall I run down like this or wave my arms like this?"

I spent a lot of the next few days shouting 'Brendan Flood come on down' and running down the stairs from the staff room and waving my arms around much to the amusement of me and my colleagues.

To be honest I was probably a bit giddy because at this time Ellen and I were preparing to get married. So as our wedding day came closer, I had more serious things to think about than 'The Price is Right'. And by the time we returned from honeymoon I'd completely forgotten about the trip, which was just around the corner.

On my first morning back at work I took a phone call in the branch at about eleven. And the voice at the other end said:

"Is that Brendan.... Brendan Flood?"

"Yeah, yeah that's me." I replied.

"You're the leader aren't you for 'The Price is Right' trip?"

At that moment it all came back to me. The trip was the following week and it turned out that the guy I was speaking to was from Central TV and was working on the show. He carried on:

"I just wanted to check with you that all the arrangements are set and everything's fine. And you've got a good party coming have you, are they a noisy group?"

"Yeah they're great."

He carried on:

"Anyway Brendan, I just want to let you in on a secret. We always choose the leader of the group to come on down."

Fantastic. I was clenching my fist in unbridled joy at this news. But I played it cool:

"Oh right. Yeah that's fine." I said as I waved frantically to attract the attention of one of the girls on the counter. The guy from Central continued:

"Great. You will get called to 'Come on Down' but we just need to check out that you'll be able to answer a few of the questions, to check that you're reasonably price sensitive."

"Oh yeah. That's fine."

"I'll just bounce a few off you okay? What about a Ford Escort 1.3 litre 1975?"

I didn't want to blow it now so I had a proper think about it before I replied:

"Ooh, about £2,100."

"Okay, what about a Steve Davis toothbrush?" (the snooker player)

"Er ... three quid?"

"Mmm, what about a pound of carrots?"

He then proceeded to go through a list of pointless products with me earnestly giving him my answers, spurred on by the encouragement of my branch colleagues, who by now were quietly trying to listen. Eventually he came to his final question:

"Okay Brendan, how much for a pint of Scotch Mist?"

I wasn't going to be beaten by this one, and guessing it was a type of whiskey I ventured a couple of quid at which point he asked:

"Are you sure? How much for a wind up Brendan?"

"Shit."

As my colleagues collapsed in an explosion of uncontrollable mirth the reality finally dawned on me that I had been done. And well done. So well done, in fact, that it went out on Red Rose Radio, which was huge at the time, at eight o' clock in the morning. So I did briefly wonder if my stint in London had taught me anything at all.

I got hundreds of phone calls that day from amused friends and I thought it might be several years before I could live it down. But as it turned out I was being a tad optimistic. That bloody recording followed me around for ages. In fact a few years later I was lecturing for the bank at the staff training centre in Wimbledon when it cropped up.

But with our keen sense of fun and spirit at the branch we turned in impressive results and soon our tiny branch was the top performing unit in the region. Our results got me noticed by the powers that be and it was then that I was transferred up to the main branch in

Fishergate as the assistant to the new manager, Martin Poyser.

The Fishergate branch had underperformed for many years and Martin was asked to go in and sort it out. He came with a big reputation as he had previously been the bank's regional marketing director. And it was an important time for me. Martin was the first major influence on me in my professional life.

I'd been used to the way of banking where someone would come in to borrow a couple of hundred thousand, and if you couldn't tick all the boxes you'd say 'no'. But Martin proved to me that there is always a way of doing everything. If you really want to, you can always make your objectives happen. Never give up on the game plan.

He was very knowledgeable and if a deal didn't stack up for the bank, he'd be able to find a way of making it work. He would show the customer how they could cut costs, or which public body they could approach to apply for a grant. He would introduce customers to business angels who could put in capital or he would restructure the proposition so that it might work for the customer and the bank. But he never dismissed a transaction that he thought was worthwhile.

I'll always be grateful to Martin because he opened my mind to a business creativity that I had never seen before. And we worked well together. I was energetic and comfortable with customers and Martin was decisive. Over the past two decades I have come to learn that decisiveness is a leading characteristic of the most successful businessmen. We more than doubled the size of the business within a year. Several of the local major companies came to bank at Barclays in Preston and the reputation of the branch was recovered.

I was starting to wonder how long I should work for the bank. I was still enjoying the job but I always had the feeling that I'd rather be doing something else, although I wasn't entirely sure what. And when I did decide to leave Barclays in many respects I was provoked by failure.

I'd been asked to go on the annual Management Development Programme down in London. It was a three day assessment centre which involved a series of psychometric tests and an interview with the main board directors. I'd done well to get on the programme as I was one of only twelve internal candidates and twelve graduates, mostly from Oxford and Cambridge. The three days went well. And it was challenging stuff, as the successful candidates were to go on a fast track programme with the aim of reaching the main board. In all honesty I was flattered to be nominated.

A few weeks later I went to see the Personnel Manager in Preston. And in true HR tradition he bludgeoned me with a 'praise sandwich':

"Right Brendan, we've got the results of your MDP assessments. You did really well at the psychometric tests and scored very highly indeed,"... but ... *"the interview comments were that you hide your light under a bushel."*
Ah. *"But on the whole you gave an excellent account of yourself and can be pleased that you got that far."*

So I hadn't been selected then. I asked what he meant by 'hiding my light under a bushel.'

"You were a bit too modest Brendan. You need to show more confidence."

It seemed to me that I hadn't boasted enough. That's what I noticed about the public school lads who had come through. They had come out of university with a false bravado that I hadn't learnt. I've learnt it now!

But my nous had been beaten by their bravado and name dropping it seemed, and that was that. The sense of how I'd been judged had turned me off. I didn't really want to work for a bank that judged people more by background and arrogance so I decided to leave. It might have been belligerent pride that pushed me, but that very moment made me want to show that I was capable of being a board director at Barclays. And if I wasn't going to do it there I'd just go and do it somewhere else.

I know that I had learnt a lot in the bank and benefitted from a really diverse education in business. But I thought that at twenty six I was now ready to make my own decisions and I wanted to work for myself. But I wasn't in a position where I could set up my own business and I needed an opportunity to prove myself.

So I went to see a chap called Martin Barlow who owned Laund Estates, a house building business based in Bolton. I'd known Martin for years and had recently done business with him and we'd always got on well. When I told him that I was getting itchy feet he suggested that I go and work with him. He offered to double my wages at the bank and a BMW.

It was a pretty hard offer to turn down. And so I abandoned the secure world of banking to learn more about property.

3

From Small Acorns

1988 – 2006

'An organization's ability to learn, and translate that learning into action rapidly, is the ultimate competitive advantage.' Jack Welch

I didn't see leaving the bank as a particularly daunting step. For a start I'd been fired up by my rejection on the fast track programme and I had bags of confidence that I could make a success of myself in the big wide world. And then of course there was my increased salary. I had just married Ellen in 1986 and the pressure was increasing for me to think more like a provider.

I think Martin had seen enough of me to know that he wasn't taking a risk. When I was at Barclays we had bailed him out at one time and the move was ideal for me.

Ellen and I were starting to work our way up the property ladder and we were no longer just working for ourselves. Our son Kevin was born not long after I joined Martin and so the extra cash was much needed.

I already knew enough about property from the financing side through my work at the bank and particularly under the guidance of Martin Poyser. So I knew what was required to put a deal together from the point of view of the funders but I still had a lot to learn about the nuances and personalities within the property game.

Laund was pretty active during that period and I took the opportunity to learn not only about house building, but also industrial and commercial development which awakened more curiosity in me. We did several projects in the North West over the next couple of years, such as the Carrs Industrial Estate in Haslingdon.

It was while I was working with Martin that my path first crossed Barry Kilby's. Laund had been appointed to put up Scapa's head office in Blackburn. We built the new head office and leased Scapa's old offices to Barry's then company Europrint. Barry was doing quite well for himself at that time. I knew he was a Burnley fan but it was a good six years before he made his move to take over the club. It was then that the club started to finally shake off the misery of the eighties and it was no coincidence that it was under Barry's stewardship. But at the beginning of the nineties his profile was still very low as far as Burnley Football Club was concerned and he was concentrating on building up his business.

It was fascinating for me to be working with a property guy, having spent all my time previously working within the restricted environment of Barclays. And Martin was an old fashioned property developer, the type that had the perennial belief that land would always go up in value. He preferred to borrow as much as he could against the land, which is classically known as pawn broking in the property world. His main strength was his grim determination. He could tough it out whenever he found himself in a difficult situation. I had already taken on board Martin Poyser's creativity and innovation in deal making. What I learnt from Martin Barlow though, was not only how to win business but also how to keep it.

Martin taught me how to get full value from every transaction. And he always warned me not to be charmed by suppliers who tried to wine and dine you. His main influence on me was to make me grittier.

In the three years that I was with Martin at Laund I learnt more about the people in the property industry. But more significantly I had begun to form the basis of my own ethos in business. I had been mentored by some good teachers and I had taken on some of their principles and characteristics. But I was now moulding my own business ideas and by the summer of 1991 I decided that I was ready to go it alone.

♦

I set up my business in the back bedroom of our home in Monton, a suburb of Manchester. We'd only moved in there the year before. In true entrepreneurial fashion, Ellen and I had bought and sold three houses in four years. I clearly had a penchant for property deals and, thankfully for me, Ellen too had a spirit of resolute adventure. We found in our first house that it grew in value pretty quickly and so we weren't frightened by the constant upheaval in agreeing to make a determined climb up the property ladder.

I knew now that my preferred sector was commercial property development, because selling one house to a buyer was as difficult as selling one large shed to a commercial occupier, but the latter is a lot more rewarding. And I was acutely aware that I was starting up in a recession, but in every downturn there are winners and losers and I was starting with a clean slate. So clean in fact that I didn't have any business lined up. I wanted to find some high value property deals, but was pragmatic enough to know that I'd have to take what I could get.

The first thing I did was to decide on a name for my business. I didn't want to call it 'Flood Properties' because people might think I was a disaster planning or insurance company! I wanted the name to reflect how I intended to do my business. I had some commercial creativity and determination, but it all needed to be knit together with a clear method. I've always had a method in everything I've tried to do. So I reached back into the dark depths of my memory of Latin classes at St Mary's College, checked in the dictionary and found the word for method. Modus. That'll do.

And then I had a very simple objective. I decided that I wanted to eventually retire with two million in the bank. That would be good enough to support a comfortable retirement and I thought that it was healthy to have an aspiration.

But I quickly discovered that being self employed is incredibly hard. As a newcomer in town I was getting no favours from professionals or entrepreneurs in the city and in many ways it was quite lonely. Pretty quickly I decided that it would help if I moved into a base in Manchester so that I could mix it with the people I needed to get to know. I took a lease on a small office in Oxford Court. It wasn't cheap but it gave me a quality environment to work in and the additional expense gave more impetus to my plans. My main intention was to find some property development, but that always takes time so I picked up some small consultancy jobs doing bits and pieces of corporate finance work to get me started. I was happy to take on any work that would pay me forty quid an hour.

And I decided that I needed to diversify. I thought I could get a bit of steady income by investing in two day nurseries with my sister Colette, one in Stockport and one in Altrincham. Ellen agreed for us to remortgage our house with the Yorkshire Building Society, and I put twenty thousand in which helped me to establish Modus and put capital into the day nurseries.

But before long both of the nurseries were struggling. They had needed more capital than we had budgeted for and we'd underestimated the fierce nature of competition in that sector. Add to that the recession reducing parents' spending power and we were in a mess.

I had quickly learnt that diversification doesn't pay, ultimately at a cost of seventy thousand pounds once we had sold off the nurseries. So I found myself at the beginning of 1993 with no business in the pipeline, no equity in my house and stacked out credit cards. I had nothing to cover my overheads and was running out of time. I sat down and worked out that I had a maximum of five months to survive. I knew that by the end of five months I would have converted a deal or packed up and got a job which I didn't want to do. But the problem was that consultancy work had dried up and development deals take a long time. And time was a commodity that I just didn't have enough of.

♦

A few years earlier I had met a Manchester businessman called Martin Abramson, a client of the law firm where Ellen was training at the time. I remembered that he had floated his company, Ronald Martin Groome, back in 1986 which realised for him over five million pounds. The reason that this sprung to mind now was that he had told me that he was keen to get into property development. And while I was working at Laund, Martin had contacted me to ask if I could let him know if any good deals came along.

I stayed in touch with Martin, partly because at the time he was one of the few wealthy people I knew so I thought at some stage he might make a useful potential backer. It also struck me that the guys who had already had the biggest influences on me were all called Martin but that didn't preoccupy me for long! I was at a pivotal stage of my business. I knew that I could find a deal and had a good eye for business but I didn't have any money. So I didn't care whether he was called Martin or Martha,

I made it my priority to arrange a meeting. I knew money was hard to come by, interest rates had climbed to twelve per cent and property was not an attractive proposition for more cautious investors, and I found myself almost begging for equity investment at times.

In one of Martin's businesses he had a young salesman working for him called Simon. The lad had only been with Martin for a few weeks but he was desperate to impress and worked every hour that God sent. And soon enough, he had gone out and done a sale for Martin of thirty five grand worth of goods. Simon was absolutely ecstatic and burst into Martin's office waving his order and saying, 'Guess what! I've done this sale, the biggest yet.' Martin could see that Simon was delighted and didn't want to let this momentous event pass without recognition. So the following day he presented him with a framed copy of the order inscribed with the words:

"WELL DONE SIMON – BUT REMEMBER THAT WAS YESTERDAY!"

Martin was extremely astute. One thing I learnt in my early meetings with him was that if you want someone to commit themselves to your business, then you need to make your offer completely irresistible. Unless it is, they won't do it, because ultimately everyone wants to look after themselves. You can be charming, likeable and clever but unless your proposition is totally irresistible then you have nothing. And as I put proposals to Martin he kept on setting the bar higher. I always gave him the option to say 'no' and I was struggling like hell to find the irresistible deal. And I desperately needed to find it soon.

I'd been working for a while on a potential development site on Tonge Moor Road in Bolton. Before Christmas I had paid a one thousand pound fee for a twelve month option to buy the site for a million. The owner could have already sold it for less but no one would pay a million. So he gave me the option. If he thought he could get a million elsewhere he would have taken it but he couldn't, so he came to me. I had secured a twelve month option and now all I needed to do was to find an occupier, find a buyer for the property investment and find a bank that would lend me the money to build it in a recession - simple. I had been trying to persuade the Co op to open a food store on the site but talks were moving very slowly and by the end of February I was getting worried.

Then I received a call from an agent based in Manchester who asked me if I was interested in talking to JH Holdings, who were looking for a suitable location in Bolton. I'd never heard of JH Holdings but I later found out that they were the owners of the retailer brand Matalan.

Matalan was an emerging business at that time and it still only had around thirty stores nationwide. I didn't have any other leads so I decided to meet with their finance director. I was confident in going to meet him but I wasn't holding any assumptions that it would be an easy discussion. One thing I did get right from the outset in my business was the quality of my preparation. My time at Barclays, and with Martin Barlow had taught me the importance of being well organised. I was confident to meet anyone, and more so if I was fully prepared.

So I did some due diligence on Matalan and went to the meeting well equipped to be able to sell the location if the numbers stacked up. And in a slightly bizarre situation, I was privy to the finances of a growing national brand, and they didn't have the faintest idea about mine. If they had, maybe I wouldn't have got a meeting in the first place. They had demonstrated their ability to pay without me demonstrating my ability to build! But they knew that I held the option on the land and in property possession is nine tenths of the law.

So I had a tenant lined up. That was the easy bit. The next thing I had to do was to persuade a bank to lend me the money. I was pinning my hopes on the British Linen

Bank, which later became the Bank of Scotland, then HBOS, then Lloyds, then the taxpayer. But at the time it was British Linen who were active in the development sector. The total project costs including the land, construction costs and finance were two million pounds, and the bank agreed to lend me 1.7 million, but only if I had the building pre sold to an investor.

I knew that virtually the only buyers in this market were the institutions where there was still an appetite to invest. I managed to get an agreement to buy the completed development from the Prudential for a shade over 2.4 million pounds. All I needed now was to raise the three hundred thousand needed to obtain the bank's advance.

So at last I had my irresistible proposition. With tightly drawn documentation and covenants I simply had to find three hundred thousand pounds to make four hundred thousand profit. It was time to go back to see Martin Abramson. I knew the deal had to be perfect for Martin. But now I could show him that I had the tenant, I had the bank onside and I had a buyer. In return for his backing I offered Martin half of the profit and that was irresistible.

Martin agreed and the deal went through. And it was just in the nick of time for me. The relief was enormous. I had survived. Twelve months later I arrived home clutching a cheque for two hundred thousand pounds and Ellen and I had a party!

I was in business and Modus was established.

♦

Throughout the nineties we operated purely as a trader and developer and by 2000 we employed about twenty staff. We had been very successful in the region, doing small to medium sized projects for the retail sector. But as our name grew we had ever more enquiries and towards the end of 2002 we became involved in a large scale shopping development in Wigan. Initially I was cautious about taking on such a large and riskier project but we managed to sell the development in it's infancy to a company called Wilson Bowden, which is now owned by Barratt. But as it turned out after twelve months Wilson Bowden decided that the project wasn't for them, so by default we had to carry on with the project on our own. This represented something of a crossroads. We had been active in completing provincial town shopping centres with ten to fifteen new shops, but was now the time to move into the large scale new build shopping centre market?

The main considerations were the timescale of completing such a big development, the capital needed to fulfil the contract and the level of debt required. We decided to spend time building up relationships with the big retailers including the likes of Marks and Spencer, Debenhams and Next and that would raise our profile in the sector so that we would become trusted. We also decided to stay in the top two hundred towns nationally and started to recruit more and more people to resource it, building up a national development team of about fifty staff, with offices in London, Birmingham, Lincolnshire and Manchester.

Over time we became a sought after development team. In all our developments we had our Unique Features and Opening plan (UFO). We were innovative and more entrepreneurial than the London based public companies and over the next four years that gave us a real edge in the market.

While all this was going on I started to look for more co-investors to work with and I opened a fund management business, bringing in David Lockhart from the Bank of Scotland and Peter Macfarlane, whose background was property. They became a very strong team, forming the asset management company which is branded as Spectrum. We created several investment funds bringing in about thirty co-investors.

We were realising profits well in excess of my budgets which then encouraged me to diversify more because property has its ups and downs. We went on to make four investments in other sectors, including Passion for Perfume, a retail business I was keen to grow. We were scaling a lot of sectors and our brand was becoming nationally stronger, driven by our courage and innovation.

And on a personal front, by 2006 Burnley Football Club had fallen into the category of non- property investment, albeit the preparation I made and the due diligence I conducted reflected a decision made very much with the heart.

4

Welcome to the Reality Son

December 2006 – May 2007

'The important thing is not to stop questioning.'
Albert Einstein

So how do you replicate business success at a football club? That's the million dollar question. In the case of one or two Premiership outfits the opening strategy seems to be to throw tens of millions at it. But that isn't comparing like for like. You don't make a success of any other business simply by making an unsustainable amount of capital expenditure on day one.

I've long since held the belief that you need to develop your own commercial ethos, have a carefully thought out strategy and a clear understanding of your own identity. And that applies equally to business and sport. Unless you have worked through all three of these cornerstones you might as well just open a franchise.

But in lots of ways football is different. In what other business would you run your salary bill at a hundred per cent of turnover or give a nineteen year old a one thousand per cent wage rise? It isn't all just befuddled commercial principles which make football different though. Historically, for many investors it is simply a labour of love. But when the Premiership arrived on the back of Sky's rebranding of the game everything changed. For sure the love is still there but for any well organised, ambitious club that reaches the Premiership, the prize is now the long term financial stability and health of the club. That is providing you continue with the principles and organisation which got you there in the first place. But it isn't easy as some fans become dazzled by the lights and get over excited.

I have learnt that it takes years to build a strong business and football clubs are no different. But for a club the size of Burnley to succeed, or Bolton or Wigan for that matter, it needs an extra special effort, with no stone unturned. Everybody needs to be on board with what you're doing. And when I joined the board at the end of 2006 I was ready to do my bit.

At my first Burnley Football Club board meeting I had been disappointed by the mood of resignation in the room. The overriding consensus seemed to me to be that we were in a division too high where we couldn't hold our own for much longer, and that was when we were sitting fourth in the league table!

My emotion as a fan was to push for the club to become a small fish in the big pond, rather than to accept inevitable relegation and be a big fish in a small pond.

There was something of an aftershock from the board meeting as talk of new investment circulated. There was a lot of reaction from the within the club and people who had worked at Turf Moor for many years were thinking, 'Hang on, there's something going on here.' Dave Edmondson, the chief executive, was trumpeting my arrival, telling the staff that now I was here I'd start to sort things out. No pressure there then! I know that Dave himself had felt a bit unloved and hadn't always enjoyed as much respect from the board as he deserved, so he was also keen to see if there would be a noticeable change.

But the biggest reaction of all was from the manager, Steve Cotterill. I'd shared a drink with Steve after the great pie debate at the AGM and I'd given him my business card. About a week later he rang me at work. This was the first of what soon became a daily phone call. Initially he was curious to see who this new director was and he had started to hear from Barry Kilby that I was prepared to back the wages bill and maybe even provide a budget for new players.

Consequently Steve wanted to build a strong working relationship with me. He often likened our relationship to the one he had with the chairman down at Cheltenham Town, where they were pals as well as chairman and manager. As we were both in our forties we had enough in common to get on well.

At first it was a totally positive relationship where we were both on the same agenda. The target was quite simply to improve the team. But it wasn't long before the first big worry cropped up. Andy Gray, our centre forward, had been injured against Leeds United the previous week. Nothing surprising in that of course but it was a real blow to the team. Andy was our main striker and had scored ten goals before Christmas. He was working very hard and was having one of his best seasons and he was one of the main reasons we were sitting in a play-off spot. But it was blindingly obvious that we didn't have any real back up for Andy, even though the young Kyle Lafferty scored twice when he was deputising in a 2-2 draw with Sunderland. We had high hopes for Kyle but he was far from ready to lead the line.

Steve had a list of suggestions about life at the club that he wanted to change, and he often seemed to be in a hurry to resolve them. He's a very bright guy but it appeared to me that he had become frustrated with the club as he was in his third year and was impatient for success at Burnley. But to go with it he has a massive amount of nervous energy. And at the time a lot of it was positive; he wanted to make things better at the club and he had huge personal ambition. He was absolutely desperate to do well. However, one of Steve's more unusual wishes was to move the away supporters from behind the goals in the Cricket Field Stand. He made it clear to me that this was one of his principle concerns as soon as I arrived. Steve always believed that when the away team brought a lot of fans they could suck the ball into the net! I could see what he meant but I have to refute it on the evidence of our Carling Cup semi-final this year. When Pavlyuchenko scored his late, late goal, it was almost in spite of the Spurs fans blowing waves of vitriol in the faces of their embattled players.

But Steve was convinced that he was right. And after the draw with Sunderland he held that game up as irrefutable proof of his theory. To be fair, we were 2-0 up with eleven minutes to go and when they pulled a goal back you could see their 3,500 fans take a collective sharp intake of breath. But I think their injury time equaliser was more to do with David Connolly's unstoppable rocket than the industrial strength lungs of a mob of Black Cats. Otherwise, as well as scoring, one of them would surely have swallowed Danny Coyne after sucking him through the net into the away end vacuum! Having said that I knew Steve had a lot of sympathy on this point from some of our fans.

When they had pulled one goal back, the Sunderland fans had really got going. Steve would, from time to time, relate back to that match, to illustrate how difficult it was to play against teams with a big following when they started to get some momentum. Steve was quite passionate about this. Coincidentally it was at about this time that we announced plans to redevelop the ground. I think subconsciously, while I couldn't see that Steve's ball sucking theory was our most pressing issue, I did want to please him and so I might have pushed the development sooner than planned. And it soon became one of Steve's weekly questions:

"How are we going on with the ground redevelopment and moving the away fans Bren?"

Of course the redevelopment remains an exciting part of our plans for the future. But I also had one very keen eye on what was going on here and now. In the first four games since I joined the board we had drawn three and lost one, scoring three goals in total. So I was desperate for us to get a win and my mind was becoming clearer by the day about the striker situation.

♦

Shortly after the Sunderland match we had a trip to Barnsley on Boxing Day. I think Barnsley as a town is similar in its make-up to Burnley because of the pride in, and ultimate loss of, the mining industry. Like us, the people there have learned to be resilient in the face of difficulty and appreciative of any good that comes their way. It's a club where they are very hospitable and welcoming in the boardroom.

On the pitch we bombarded them for most of the game but just couldn't score. Then Barnsley scored a goal and we lost 1-0. Even though we'd spent a lot of the game in their half I thought we looked a bit leaderless at the back. We didn't seem to have anyone organising the defence on the rare occasions that we were under attack. So it wasn't really a surprise when they scored. It wasn't exactly the merriest way to round off Christmas but then, for some unfathomable reason, I think Boxing Day is often that way for Burnley fans. After the game almost everyone made a fairly quick escape. But I was in a mood to stick around and have a couple of drinks and I got talking to one of the Barnsley directors called Barry Taylor. He's one of the long established directors there, Barnsley through and through. He was on the board when they were in the Premiership and he always seems to have a smile on his face. As we began to chat I could sense that Barry was going to provide me with the benefit of his experience.

He asked me how long I'd been on the Burnley board and when I replied, 'About a month,' he looked at me with a glint in his bespectacled eyes and in his broad Yorkshire accent said:

"Let me give you some advice lad. If ever a fan approaches you on the street and wants to ask you a few things about the club, and tell you what you should do, and how you should change things, ask 'em, 'Ave they got a season ticket?'" At this point jabbing his finger and raising his eyebrows as he continued, *"and if they aven't, tell 'em to bugger off!"*

Barry explained that he only answers question from people who have season tickets, because he believes that they are, in effect, members of the club and they deserve a response:

"That's it, I won't answer anyone else."

And luckily for me he had a second piece of advice:

"Whatever you do son, don't put any money into the club."

"Why not?"

"Because you're better off going to Scarborough and pissing in te't sea!"

At that very moment in time I didn't really need that bit of advice. But we carried on chatting and he told me about how life had been for Barnsley in the Premier division and how they seem to have just floundered since and what their ambitions were now. It made me think that, even though we were a club and a town similar to them, that we could do better than Barnsley. I believed that they had already fully spent their ambition whereas we haven't yet. I came away from Oakwell, taking heed of Barry's advice but wanting more for our club. But as we left the deserted Oakwell stadium, stood silent behind us, it sank in that we were leaving again with no points.

And after the last game of 2006 there was still no sign of improvement on the pitch, in fact it was getting worse.

We lost 2-0 at Hull, who were close to the bottom at the time, and we could have been playing until Easter without scoring as far as I could see. As we moved into the January transfer window Steve was now desperate to get a striker to replace Andy Gray; so most of my phone calls in early January were about which strikers Steve would like. He always wanted to sign players he had watched several times and he didn't like to take too much of a risk on players he didn't know well. This is good management but inevitably it directed his interest to more established players.

My preference was really to get younger players but Steve was always after experience. He often said to me:

"It's alright having players who may become great one day but we need someone now. I'm the manager and I might run out of time."

It's true that managers do run out of time, but we needed a medium term plan with a predominance of younger players. Those words revealed a lot about Steve's psyche, in a lot of ways he was quite cautious. He watched football for every hour of the day and he wasn't particularly interested in anything else. And he had a genuine desire to become England's manager, which arguably was a bit over ambitious at the time, particularly as we had just gone on a six match winless streak. But he really believed that one day he'd become the England manager. And that demonstrated to me that Steve wasn't committed to Burnley indefinitely, but he was doing time until he received a Premiership offer. I never felt that he was with us for the long haul. For Steve it was always going to be a stepping stone to something else.

Steve and I had started to get to know each other pretty well and from an early stage I made a point of ringing him before and after each game to try to give him some support. That is something that the chairman or one of the directors should do in most clubs, because the manager needs someone to tell him he's doing a good job too. That relationship is vital in any football club. Managers need to have support and feedback, whether it's good or bad. So I made it my job to do that; probably because I was more of a peer with Steve in terms of age than anyone else on the board. And I enjoyed his passion for football.

Steve dearly wanted Burnley to progress but he didn't want to gamble further on younger players. He felt that in Kyle Lafferty and Chris McCann we had made enough of an investment in young players and beyond that he needed to have an experienced side. So Steve's choice of strikers ultimately came down to him wanting to make a forthright bid for Ade Akinbiyi, who was at Sheffield United and wasn't getting a game at the time. Ade had been successful at Burnley with Steve previously, so for the manager he ticked all the boxes.

Neil Warnock at Sheffield United was willing to sell Ade, so it was an easy deal to do and it was completed in a couple of phone calls. Ade was delighted too; he liked Burnley and felt wanted here. He's very much a player that needs to be loved by the fans and Steve had a lot of belief in him. So within a week of the transfer window opening we had bought Ade back for seven hundred and fifty thousand.

Steve was relieved to introduce a striker to cover for Andy Gray and at the press conference he publicly thanked me for supporting him on that deal. He had a strong sense of gratitude about him that was always present in our relationship; he always thanked me for my support, where appropriate, which I appreciated. He had obviously been brought up with good manners, which was an endearing quality.

So we had Ade back, but it was soon evident from a very long distance that he was all top heavy. He hadn't been in the team at Sheffield and had clearly been spending all his time in the gym. In his first few matches back he didn't really settle into his stride. He was as powerful as ever and if he ran towards you, you would most probably fear for your life, but he couldn't turn quickly and as he ran towards the goal all the fans on the front row appeared to dive for cover. He covered twice as much ground as everyone else but as his legs became tired it took him a lot longer. So Steve started working on him, banning him from the gym and getting him running and turning. There was no sign of Andy Gray coming back quickly, and so a lot was resting on Ade's colossal shoulders. But he'd been a great player for us before so there was no reason why he couldn't do it again.

◆

For the past few years at Modus I had organised a big corporate skiing trip every January. The idea was for us to take forty or so business partners and professionals that we use; bankers, lawyers and corporate finance guys. It's always a fun event, a chance for us to start off the year by thanking people who have helped us, strengthen key relationships, get some good skiing done and have a few beers. But when I went this time I had a bit more to worry about. The first cause for concern was the unimpressive run of results we'd had at Burnley since I had become a director. We'd signed Ade which was good, but I had hoped to see some results on the pitch, sooner rather than later. And there was something else going on, in the business world, which I couldn't quite put my finger on. The economic wind was quietly changing direction.

We set off for a week in Majeve, about forty five of us, looking forward to the skiing and the après-ski. As it turned out, it was a challenging week for me in a number of respects. For a start, when we arrived, all we could see was grass! Evidently the biggest problem wasn't yet the looming credit crunch, it was global warming. At that time people were talking about it every week and as I looked out at the green and brown view in front of me I was thinking, 'Christ, we may never be able to ski again!'

And because there was less snow around it gave us more opportunity to talk. I always took the opportunity to work my way around the group, there were a wide range of senior figures attached to the property industry and they were a good barometer for how the corporate community felt back home.

2006 had been a spectacular year in the market, but this time I could sense that there was a different atmosphere to the previous year. Last year the mood had been 'Let's do the deals, let's expand'. It was dynamic and fearless. But this time there was a distinct air of reticence. It was like watching a balloon deflating in front of me. I could feel that there was a softening, so I grabbed a few of my key guys to take them for a coffee. I particularly wanted to speak to Peter McFarlane and David Lockhart from my asset management team at Modus.

The guys weren't as convinced about the change in sentiment as I was so I relied on my instinct. We agreed that we should start to consider property disposals on some schemes and get back to cash by the middle of the year.

♦

Back at the football club Steve was trying to improve the forward line, but when I thought back to the game at Barnsley and the following few games, we clearly needed more leaders in the squad. As I had now become the principal investor at the club, I had suggested to Steve that as a pre-condition to any new signings that the individual players should be natural leaders. Strong personalities stand out and if we selected a team of captains then we would have a team with real character. From that discussion onwards I would always ask, 'Has he been a captain?' when Steve recommended any new players. And from January 2007 most of the players added to the squad had previously been captains in their recent career. We soon managed to sign Joey Gudjonsson for two hundred and fifty thousand. Steve remembered him from Leicester as a combative little midfielder with a fierce shot. So we thought he could help us to protect the defence and provide some goals. Then we started to look around for a dominant centre half. We became aware that Steve Caldwell up at Sunderland was potentially available. I knew that he was a very capable centre back and their club captain during the previous year. There were rumours of a couple of players up there who weren't happy, and Steve was one of them. He no longer wanted to be at Sunderland and so at five minutes to midnight on the last day of the transfer window we brought him to Burnley for four hundred thousand pounds.

We immediately installed Steve as our team captain. To some extent we had a vacancy because the job had been moved around during the season. At the start it was Wayne Thomas but he kept getting booked or sent off, so the captaincy was then shared between John McGreal and Frank Sinclair. But now with Steve we had clarity of leadership on the field. And in the transfer window we had made three significant acquisitions.

Like most leaders, Steve Caldwell soon showed that he had a strong personality. And I got the feeling that, as time went by, a tense atmosphere had started to build up between our manager and captain. Steve Caldwell wasn't frightened to voice his opinion, which the manager sometimes didn't like.

We hoped that Steve, Joey and Ade when he was fully fit, would make the impact that we were looking for. But as the weeks went on it just didn't happen. We went through the whole of February without winning a game and by the end of the month we found ourselves entrenched in the bottom half of the division and looking over our shoulders at relegation.

In the early stages of our relationship Steve appeared excited by my involvement on the board. But the more he understood me and my ambition for the club I think he started to feel an increased sense of pressure. Our miserable run of form was worrying both of us.

During this time I found Steve getting more and more concerned and sensitive about his own position until eventually one day he rang up and said:

"Look Bren, if you're going to bloody well sack me, just sack me okay!

It's hard for managers, particularly if they care passionately, which Steve did. And you'd have to be completely naive to believe that after thirteen games without a win no one is questioning your ability to do the job. I tried to reassure Steve with my response:

"No Steve, we don't want to sack you. Let's just concentrate on trying to figure out what's going wrong. What can we do better?"

In all honesty, when we had gone beyond a dozen games without winning it definitely was a worry in the boardroom. It was going to be difficult to keep supporting Steve, but we knew how hard he was trying. He was doing his best, testing out new ideas and changing the team but, for whatever reason, things weren't going our way. I wasn't sure that all the players were in harmony with Steve and I started to suspect that may have been the problem.

The malaise dragged on well into March. And it hadn't escaped my attention that in the three months since I had pledged to plough two million of my own money into the club, during which we had spent a good chunk of it, we had played seventeen games and won precisely none. Barry Taylor at Barnsley had been absolutely right. I should have gone and 'pissed it into the sea at Scarborough'. And to make matters worse game number eighteen was an away match at Preston. We just had to win it. I hate losing to Preston at any time, but at this very moment it mattered a lot more. I thought that this had to be the one where the players would come good. Preston were up in a play-off spot but that didn't necessarily mean anything, we all know that local derbies are often more about desire than ability. The build up to the match during the week was a really nervous one for our fans, players, the manager and me. I decided it was a good time to go skiing again.

♦

In actual fact I was desperately keen to see Burnley win and gutted that I might miss it at Preston. But the skiing trip had been arranged for months. It wasn't business, more of a holiday with a bunch of mates. I sent my eldest son Kevin to watch the match and arranged to check with him during the game to see how we were getting on. On the afternoon of the match, and after we'd had a thrilling day on the slopes, I was on my way back down the mountain when I noticed it was twenty past three back home and my phone hadn't gone off. So as I sat on the ski lift in Austria I decided to give Kevin a ring. He picked up straight away and all I could hear from the other end was the roar of the crowd. I nearly fell off the lift:

"Kev, have we scored? Have we scored?" His response wasn't quite as I'd hoped.

"No Preston have!" I didn't believe him:

"They can't have, I can hear the crowd dead loud!"

"I'm in the Preston end!"

Bloody Hell. The silly lad hadn't got his ticket in time so he had to sit with the PNE fans. And by the time we reached the bar a text came through telling me that Nugent had scored and we were 2-0 down. And that was the end of it. We lost 2-0 and were now eighteen games without a win.

The lads on the ski trip said that they'd never seen me so depressed. If I'm upset about a game I tend to go a bit quiet. I was that upset about it all that I went and sat outside the bar with my hood up. I was desperately down, and I brought the whole group down for an hour or two. There was no hearty humour. My mates were all with me in spirit and they'd been following Burnley's results since the beginning of the year. They knew it mattered so much to me. So while we all had pints in our hands nobody was talking. It must have looked pretty weird to the après ski crowd and the locals.

To be honest, while the gloom had lifted from the group, it was still weighing heavily on my mind by the time we went home. It was a double whammy. We'd lost to Preston and it was the eighteenth game. And if I'm honest, I'd even started to question what I'd been doing. I'd spent serious personal money and given Steve a lot of support but I started wondering if this was an area that I didn't know much about.

In my heart of hearts I felt that the team wasn't good enough. Even when I was getting pressure from Steve to get loan players in and push on, I thought that the core of the team just wasn't good enough. That was the reality that had, over the past few weeks, become painfully clear to me.

And the situation was becoming hazardous. There were nine games left in the season and we had dropped to within four points of the relegation zone. I knew that if we had the same return from the last nine games as we had from the previous eighteen we would be playing at Stockport County next season!

There was a break on the Saturday following the Preston game as it was an international weekend. It seemed too long to wait for the next game. We were just desperate to play and win to put an end to the malaise that was in danger of engulfing the club and putting a premature end to the hopes and dreams that had driven me to become involved. And what's more the next game was a home match against Luton Town, who were bottom of the league. They had dropped like a stone and hadn't picked up a good result in weeks, so surely we were going to win this one. Burnley isn't the only club whose supporters should have learned by now never to say that, but sometimes you just can't help yourself. We had to win!

This was the first match that I had taken Ellen to since I'd been involved as a director. I think she agreed to come partly because she knew how important the game had become. The atmosphere at the ground was dreadful - it was very hushed. Everybody was nervous and it was difficult for any of us the get really excited about the game. Actually, Ellen was about the only person who was excited.

Barry's wife Sonya was gesturing to Ellen and trying to persuade her to sit next to her on the front row. There's an established gentleman's club style protocol in the directors box where all the directors sit on one row and their wives sit on the row in front. Sonya's kind attempt to drag Ellen onto the front row was fruitless and we settled down to watch the match on the back row of the box, which is my usual spot.

Our disruption of the longstanding seating arrangements in the director's box was by far the most entertaining and creative moment of the afternoon. On the pitch we managed to get a 0-0 draw against the only team in the league that was in worse form than us! Their defence could have sat on the front row of the Bob Lord Stand and it would still have been 0-0.

I was talking it up to Ellen saying, 'Well it's not that bad, we made a draw. It's better than a defeat'. That was a case of stating the obvious apart from the 'it's not that bad' bit which was a lie. In truth it was bad. Very bad indeed. And I knew that I was actually just talking it up for my own benefit, particularly as Ellen was looking at me in a disturbingly pitiful way for a first-timer! She knew it had been a huge game. Deep down, I knew that this had been a disaster. Throughout the afternoon I had been getting steadily more anxious but I was trying not to show it. I had started to think that the terrible reality might be that we could really go down here.

By the Sunday morning I had begun to get a bit agitated about it all, partly I think because Ellen had been along and heightened my own sense of worry. It was preying on my mind. The team wasn't playing well and if we did go down we had already given contracts to players some of whom arguably wouldn't get us back up. I'd already invested over two million pounds and I was at the stage where I didn't want to spend any more on loan players. The advice I had received from Phil Gartside, the Bolton chairman, seven months earlier was ringing in my ears when he said:

"Remember, bad times are always just around the corner in football!"

I was staring into the abyss. This wasn't like a normal Sunday. It's usually the family's rest day. Steve often rang me after watching The Championship on ITV and we'd exchange views. But this time when he rang I had started to grit my teeth a bit. In a sense of frustration I let go of a few expletives which I hadn't done with Steve before:

"Look Steve, I could have put the ball in the net myself! We had no one following in. The crosses were coming in and there was no one there. It seems to me like nobody's going the extra yard for the fans. There's no passion. They should get angry. The players should get angry with themselves, angry at the situation and perform with some pride. And you need to let rip now because it's getting ridiculous."

It's fair to say that I was a bit terse about it. It was the first time that we'd had that tone of conversation but it had been coming. It was man chat. I had shown my teeth and Steve took the point.

The following day Steve went out on Radio Lancashire saying, 'It's time for everyone to get angry now'. He had the presence of mind to leave out the 'F's but he had obviously got himself pumped up. I was desperate for Steve and the team to have a change of luck, but I was quietly beginning to panic.

I hoped that Steve had got the players fired up as well because on the Tuesday we had a rearranged home match against Plymouth Argyle. And on the morning of the game sitting in my office I noticed a poster I'd bought on a visit to Cape Canaveral the previous year. It was a picture of the Apollo Eleven with an American flag on it and in big bold print the words:

"FAILURE IS NOT AN OPTION"

Hmmm. I picked it up and decided it might be a good motivator for our manager! So I had it framed and wrapped and got one of my staff to deliver it to Turf Moor at 5-30 pm with the instructions to hand it personally to Steve.

That was clearly the seminal moment of our season as we went on that night to give Plymouth a 4-1 thumping! Good old Plymouth always come along when we need them to allow us to win.

It felt like three wins in one game for me, I was that thrilled. I once again experienced that warm positive feeling that I'd almost forgotten. At last the players had done their bit and the light at the end of our tunnel was shining brightly.

Steve was relieved and grateful for the poster message which he had used in his pre match briefing. Maybe it had helped, but we had our first win for months and it felt fantastic.

The following Saturday we were away at Birmingham, who were top of the league at the time. It was exciting to go into the boardroom that day with a win under our belts, and the chance to spend a bit of time with the sex industry! When I met David Gold and David Sullivan it occurred to me that this was the first time I'd been in the company of such heavyweights in the sector. Stu the Perv would have been star struck. They were very friendly and had a chirpy likeable style to them which was quite appealing.

I took my pal Steve Tattersall with me. And when we arrived in the boardroom we were both dying to go to the bathroom. So we were directed to this incredibly posh lobby area behind the boardroom and into the gents, a term that is no way near adequate in describing the regal facilities that we discovered there. It was like being in the Queen's water chamber. There were marbled walls, rich deep carpets on the floor and beautiful gold taps on the sinks. Steve and I were quite taken aback by the luxury of it all, so much so that we spent an extra couple of minutes in the toilets admiring them.

My dad and Kevin went into the directors' guest lounge, where it turned out there was no food and limited drinks, while we were next door eating like kings all afternoon! And we played with real confidence as well. With ten minutes of the match to go we were holding Birmingham to a 0-0 draw. Then John Spicer, our young midfielder who up until then had promised a lot but not really delivered, had a moment of inspiration. He caught one of their centre halves in possession on the half way line and made a run towards the penalty box. And then he unleashed a shot from twenty five yards that flew into the top corner of the net. Unbelievably we'd won.

What a glorious week. Back at the club on Monday Steve was walking tall again and I was totally relieved. I still had my concerns about the mental strength of the team, but knew that they had enough in them to get us out of trouble. And in football momentum is crucial. Two weeks ago we were hurtling at break neck speed towards League One oblivion but we'd managed to stop the rot. Now we were picking up momentum the other way. Before the end of the season we beat Cardiff and West Brom, who were promoted along with Birmingham, and gave Sunderland a cracking game which we were unlucky to lose 3-2.

Steve was really pleased that he had demonstrated we could beat the top clubs in the division. We lost the final game of the season at home to Coventry which almost felt like an anti-climax, although it didn't really matter. At least we were still there in the Championship, having finished fifteenth, a slight improvement on the previous season. Now we could forget about the darkest day at Preston and get on with the rebuild.

It hadn't been the five months I'd hoped for at the club. It was clear that we needed to make some changes, but having overcome those first nineteen games I decided to stick to a tried and tested philosophy. Whenever I take over in any business or any situation I always aim to give people twelve months before I judge them. I rarely make a decision on someone before twelve months is up. Sticking with that view, whatever the outcome of the season, I wanted to give Steve the opportunity to succeed through until the following Christmas before I made a judgement.

5

Who's Michael Essien?

May - August 2007

'In the future everyone will be world famous for fifteen minutes.' Andy Warhol

In the cool light of day, it's easier to rationalise a troublesome situation than when you're right in the thick of it. It had been hard for me to put my finger on what was happening during the nineteen game winless run. For sure, we all knew that the team wasn't good enough, but for the first three months they had turned in results to get us into a play off spot. Then, from the moment I joined the board we suddenly embarked on a run of form completely deserving of relegation.

Perhaps it was just an unhappy coincidence. After all, ever since our promotion in 2000 we have always been a team of two halves, falling away with miserable dependability, usually as soon as we'd all taken our Christmas trees down. But nineteen games, that was unprecedented. We had started the run with a couple of fighting draws but somehow managed to descend into a team entirely bereft of confidence and ideas.

I had come to the conclusion that even with good organisation and a tough mentality we could only expect this team to win maybe six or seven out of nineteen. The Championship is a tough division to shine in but our squad was mid table at the best and it was certain to be difficult again the following season. The team obviously needed more pace and strength. At the back we were reasonably solid, apart from the occasional spectacular gaff. But in midfield we had too much dynamo and not enough power. We had Wade Elliot, Joey Gudjonsson, Alan Mahon and James O'Connor. The Clarets Mad fans called it 'The Land of the Midgets!' That was maybe a bit harsh but not wholly inaccurate. Jon Harley at left back wasn't a giant either. Clearly we did need more height all round.

And up front we had really struggled. Andy Gray had been injured, Kyle Lafferty had flattered but hadn't scored many, and in all honesty, Ade had underperformed since he returned.

When you're on the board you have to trust the manager's judgement. We all make mistakes and sometimes events beyond our control, like injuries, can make a signing look poorly judged. But by and large a manager will stand or fall by the quality of his signings. Having said all that, over the past couple of years I have become much more informed about the process of buying players myself. I have built up some knowledge of the industry and got to know several agents and the football staff at other clubs so now I'm always networking for the manager to help him source new players. At that time I was principally led by Steve's recommendations and was happy to take his view.

And Steve Cotterill also required a bit of moral support from time to time. He needed to feel a good level of respect to be happy. He wanted to be seen in the same light as he sees himself, as a Premiership manager in the making. Whether Steve's opinion of himself at the time was right or wrong only time will tell. But in many ways managing a football team is no different to managing a team in an office. You need a strong leader who can soak up the pressure.

During that nineteen game run Steve genuinely tried his best, but he wasn't always entirely noble in the way he took the pressure and I think that made the players more nervous at times. It didn't help me either, as I noticed my grip on the posh white seats started to get tighter by the game!

♦

So by the end of the 2006/2007 we had decided that the team wasn't powerful enough. But I also quickly worked out that the business wasn't strong enough in terms of the football club. Commercially the figures were dropping and that was at a relatively buoyant time in the economy. In a small part that reflected the decline in the team's performance but a lot of the commercial activity can be protected from fluctuating results on the pitch. I felt that Dave Edmondson, the chief executive, was a popular and gifted spokesman but maybe not a natural chief executive. He had done a lot for the club over the past couple of years. Dave was instrumental in getting a one million pound grant for us to develop the hospitality facilities in the Jimmy McIlroy Stand. That had bemused me at the time because there was a feeling on the board that we shouldn't take the grant because we were concerned that it would bring a non refundable VAT bill of £70,000 with it, and we'd have to find the cash for that! To me it was too good an opportunity. The commercial revenue that the project would generate would eat up any VAT liability within a year. I really don't think that Dave got the respect he deserved for that. But in other areas perhaps he wasn't getting involved enough in the detail of the club's operations and in some ways the club was frightened to market itself in business terms.

There were some very good people within the club who

needed to be rewarded and motivated to improve the business.

I had a chat with Dave Edmondson, because I already knew that he was ready to move on and do his own thing. And so at the beginning of the close season he stepped down, but agreed to stay on for a while to help me on the ground development side (I was still worried about the away fans sucking the ball into the net). It was right for Dave. Not only had he not always enjoyed the respect from the Board, but he'd also been on the end of some unfair flak from the fans, because people thought that he was a Blackburn fan, but even so he didn't deserve that criticism.

At the next board meeting in early June the directors set about discussing various candidates and a six figure salary for the vacant CEO position. There was one candidate that everybody seemed keen on. He was a senior director at Trevor Hemmings' business in Blackpool, part of the Center Parks group. Everyone thought he was appropriate, so Barry and I went to meet him.

He seemed to be a capable chap but after our meeting I really didn't think he was right for us so I said:

"Look Barry, I've got over three million in the club and over the next few years I'll probably end up investing a further four to five million."

Every business that I'd ever got involved in, I had made sure I was very involved in the detail so I carried on:

"I don't feel close enough to the business here Barry. I want to understand the people at our club better than I do. Do you have any problem with me becoming more involved in the operations and getting stuck in?"

I discussed at length with Barry the option of me effectively doing the work of the CEO for the time being. But when it was put to the board there were a lot of concerns that I couldn't afford to commit the time.

However I knew that I would make the time somehow and I was given the title of Operations Director.

♦

In all fairness there was an awful lot going on at that time in the business world. It was only a few months after the point when I'd noticed a change in the wind, and it was a time to make sure that Modus was remaining strong and nimble enough to react quickly to what was happening in the market.

The last twelve months had been fantastic for us at Modus, we'd gained a lot of respect and a higher profile in the industry and we had been put up for a couple of national awards. There was one in Manchester that I had been nominated for. I had an invitation to go to the Property Week awards evening to be held at the Radisson Manchester, where I had been put forward for the Property Personality of the Year. I couldn't go because I was already committed to do a council presentation on the same night and in any case I assumed that I hadn't won it. John Whittaker, the chap who'd built up Peel Holdings, the owner of the Trafford Centre, was up for it along with a couple of other top candidates. So I politely declined and thought no more about it.

It was a typically tedious night at the council meeting and when I got home at about eleven I sat down in the kitchen with a cup of tea. Then all of a sudden I started getting texts saying, 'Well done Brendan' and 'You deserve it'. I got about a dozen of these and wondered what was going on. Then it came to me. Oh no – it must be the Property Week night! What I didn't know was that the awards were voted for on the night on a buzzer system and when some guy stood up and said, 'The winner is Brendan Flood' everyone clapped, waited and no one got up. What's more, when he asked if any of my team were there, he was met by a sea of faces looking blank until someone at the back shouted 'No'. A pal of mine said it looked super cool that I wasn't there to see if I'd won but actually I was horrified to have missed it.

But I have to admit that I did have a bit of form. In May the Property Industry dinner was held in London to raise money for the Variety Club. It's not something I'd ever been to and I can honestly say that I didn't actually know when it was. I'd just had a game of tennis at the David Lloyd club in Bolton and I was about to go home when I had a phone call from a chap I know in the business which began:

"Brendan, where are you?

"In Bolton, why where are you?" I replied.

"Variety Club Property Dinner in London, and guess what, you're up for Entrepreneur of the Year!"

I had no idea that I was anywhere near being selected. And if I was going to win surely they would have made sure I was there, so I asked:

"Who else is in the final?"

The answer left me cold:

"Sir Tom Hunter and Sir Richard Branson."

I was stunned. Sir Tom Hunter, Sir Richard Branson ... and me. This was one of those moments when you feel simultaneously like you might be missing something amazing or you might end up in the Tower. It wasn't quite the twenty first century version of thumbing your nose at two Knights of the Realm but at the very least it might be embarrassing. I had a brief moment of panic. Nobody had told me I was in the final even.

Thankfully the voters on the night had some recognition of greatness, or certainly some decorum and sense of social status and I didn't win. That was a relief. I probably won't make it to a hundred but if I do I don't want to miss out on the Queen's telegram on the grounds of insubordination.

Admittedly I had started to feel nervous that I was making a habit of missing awards dinners. I don't really know why, but I guess it was the uncertainty of not knowing how far you can go before people in your sector think you don't care. In truth there was one award that we all at Modus really wanted, the Estates Gazette Property Company of the Year. The award is the principal prize in the industry and it's seen as an honour for everything that you're doing as a business. It's very team orientated and we desperately wanted our team to win. We'd worked really hard to undertake complicated large scale projects and our competitors were trying to keep up with the ideas that we had introduced into the industry, both in terms of marketing flare, building finishes and relationship management.

We were in the final of Retail Developer of the Year and were up against Grosvenor, the Duke of Westminster's company, and we won. But more importantly we were also in the final of the Property Company of the Year award along with British Land and Land Securities. When we won both awards I was absolutely delighted. The latter was the only award that the whole business really wanted to win. There was a big crowd of us down at the presentation and the team was ecstatic. We had a fantastic late night out in London and I thought it was the best way to thank them all. We had a well thought of team at Modus with creative instinct and impressive delivery skills. They were all good with people and that gave us another edge.

But while we were getting national recognition for what had gone before, I was starting to become more aware of what was happening now. Some of the properties which we had planned to dispose of after the skiing trip in spring were taking time to sell. All the bids for one portfolio which we jointly owned with the Royal Bank of Scotland were in by the beginning of May, and we had received an offer from a wealthy Asian family who were planning to put it into a private family trust. It was the best offer we had and we agreed the terms of the deal. But within a month the family were struggling with progressing their bank funding even after it had been confirmed - and so the transaction was delayed. The only way we could complete was to absorb a big price reduction which we refused to do. I knew by now that this transaction was a good measure of how the market was turning, we didn't anticipate global meltdown but business was certainly getting more difficult.

Then a funny thing happened to me on the way to the office one day in June. We had a facility agreed with the Anglo Irish Bank to fund a one hundred and seventy million pound scheme in Wakefield. It was a high quality deal and the proposed development was already pre-let to the likes of Sainsbury's, H & M and Debenhams. We and the vendors were happily going forward to start drawing down the bank facility within a week when I received a call from the bank. The chief executive of Anglo Irish was coming to Manchester specifically to meet me to talk about the Wakefield development. This was short notice to say the least.

So a couple of hours later I was in the boardroom of the Anglo Irish Bank on a beautiful sunny day and with a grandiose rooftop view of the city of Manchester. As I looked out over the city, the chief executive sat in front of me. He wasn't openly sharing his thoughts but there was obviously a worry in his mind about the banking market. I could tell that the Anglo Irish had started to feel concerned about their property exposure as he asked me for my thoughts on the market and if I believed there was any risk of us not securing enough occupiers to fill the shopping centre. At the end of the meeting he said that he'd ring me soon to confirm when the first tranche of the facility could be released.

True to his word he rang me as I walked back to the Modus offices to confirm that we could go ahead. As I carried on walking I thought, 'that was a bit odd, and certainly unusual'. This was the largest development scheme in Yorkshire and a huge loan in a high quality location and I hadn't had a doubtful tap on the shoulder like that for over ten years. That did give me a slight shiver.

◆

As the summer of 2007 progressed I was still feeling ever more optimistic on the football front and slightly more pessimistic on the business front. And I was really up for improving the standards of business at Burnley Football Club. I wanted us to be a premier set up off the field to support what we were trying to achieve on it. So at the next board meeting I presented a passionately scripted "Vision Document" of how I felt we could improve the club in all areas. It was based on financial research that I had done on other role models for Burnley, namely Reading, Bolton Wanderers and Wigan Athletic. I was trying to demonstrate how we could achieve their status in terms of ground development and commercial improvements and how we could become stronger by reviving our youth policy and make progress both on and off the pitch year by year. I explained that I intended to become more active on a day to day basis. And so as a measure of my commitment I agreed to allocate two days a week to the club during June and July.

I spent a lot of the next few weeks with the staff at Burnley, putting the kettle on and meeting the staff. There were about ninety or so non-playing staff at the club and I wanted to get to know all of them. It soon became clear to me that the vast majority of the staff were good people and if we worked harder on motivating them we could really have a successful club. But like most sizeable businesses there were some internal politics that needed sorting out. I wanted to grow an atmosphere of togetherness as soon as possible. We needed to have everyone pulling in the same direction if we were going to have a decent chance of success.

So I called a senior management team meeting of Chris Gibson, the hospitality manager, Cathy Pickup the club secretary, Doug Metcalf, ground facilities, and our financial controller Ken Stout. This was an experienced management team who I knew could help to create a team mindset. When I had been doing a tour around the club a common theme that kept on coming back to me was that the frayed lines of communication had obviously hampered the progress of each department, and the operation as a whole. That had been a problem for Dave Edmondson and it was a major priority for us to resolve.

As we were creating a stronger team ethos in the club we quickly introduced a bonus structure for managers in the retail, hospitality and commercial divisions. I was keen to give credit and thanks where it was due and to help the staff to understand how their contribution strengthens the whole business, and ultimately resources to improve the football team. To motivate all staff I introduced staff awards which were presented at the club's Player of the Year events. It gave everyone an opportunity to be noticed.

Then Barry and I got involved with the youth academy. There is a huge amount of pride in the history of our young player development, and in the seventies our conveyor belt of talent was envied throughout the league. And we've all said that a thousand times. But the financial pressures of football at anything below the very top level are such that people want success immediately. Whether it's staying in the Premiership or getting promoted from the Championship every manager wants his quota of experienced players who can bring results today.

The biggest clubs invariably snap up the best young players but there are always a few that will slip through their nets. We always have the first chance to work with local youngsters. But the fact of the matter is that if Burnley is to get back to the glory days of the sixties and seventies, or even compete at the highest level then we will have to nurture our own talent. We can't simply buy our way to the top. And in any case, where's the real reward in buying success?

So we went to our Centre of Excellence and sat down with Geoff Taylor, Terry Pashley and Vince Overson. Geoff, Terry and Vince are all big guys in heart and stature and they love Burnley football club. But like other areas of the club they hadn't had much attention. We only had to ask one question to discover that the Centre of Excellence badly needed physical investment, manpower resource and the flexibility of funding to be able to attract better players. We asked which players had passed through the club and gone on to succeed elsewhere. Geoff replied:

"Matt Derbyshire was here for a week and we weren't able to sign him."

That stuck in the gullet a little as Matt quickly went on to become a rising star just down the road at Blackburn Rovers.

"And Michael Essien had a trial for a few days but we didn't sign him either."

What? One of the best players at the last World Cup and the lynchpin of Chelsea's recent success had trained with us first but we hadn't signed him. And why was that? Because the club policy was that we wouldn't pay more than sixty pounds a week for an apprentice! Here the recurring theme came up and smacked me between the eyes. We refused to pay more than sixty pounds a week for Michael Essien, because there was no clear line of communication to enable our guys to make an exception to the policy.

The lack of any proper communication link between our Centre of Excellence and the Board was symptomatic of the whole club. It was holding the club back. Both directors and staff had been devastated and exhausted by the years of struggling. The ITV Digital cash crisis had frozen the club and hampered the ability to speculate in any department. Barry had done a fantastic job at the head of the club, but just like on the pitch, we also needed to fill our off-field operation with motivated leaders.

During the close season we had a lot of publicity for the proposed redevelopment of the ground. And I had for some time planned to contact one of my childhood heroes who I dearly wanted to bring back to Turf Moor at some stage. Paul Fletcher was, for me, the most experienced CEO in the business and had built a huge reputation in stadium development. He had masterminded the McAlpine Stadium in Huddersfield before negotiating the naming rights for the Reebok in Bolton. Later he was asked to manage the new Wembley Stadium project and famously walked out after a year and a half, saying that he wanted to spend more time with his family in the beautiful North! Who can blame him as Wembley later became a major political battle when funding ran out at a critical stage. Latterly Paul was working at Coventry City as their chief executive where he was recruited to manage the development of the Ricoh Arena.

I rang Paul and then went to see him down at Coventry where I was really impressed by his achievements there. I enjoyed spending time with Paul. He's a very likeable character. He's an engaging after dinner speaker and a strong communicator with a good team ethos. Paul has a passion for Burnley, and I knew that it was critical to get good communicators into the club and he was ideal. He still lived in Rawtenstall but was committed at Coventry at the time so I knew he wouldn't be able to come to Turf Moor straight away, but we agreed to keep in touch.

♦

The start of the 2007/2008 season was preceded by incessant phone calls from Steve as we tried to assemble a better team. We agreed that in the main we needed leaders, and faster, more powerful players with more height in midfield. When you looked around at the best sides in our division, as well as football ability, they all had strength and pace. We also needed another keeper because Danny Coyne had gone. And when Steve rang me to say he could get Gabor Kiraly I had to think for a minute before I realised he was the one with the baggy tracksuit bottoms at Crystal Palace. He did appeal to me because he had always been spectacular when I saw him, and Steve was keen to sign him so we offered him a two year contract.

And we definitely needed more flair up front. Andy Gray was coming back from injury and we had Ade and Kyle as well. But we both felt that we needed someone with a bit more guile and the ability to score and create. At about that time it had come to most Burnley fans attention that an interesting bi-product of Leeds relegation to League One was that Robbie Blake had gone down with them. And while Leeds had a lot of players who would fit well in the lower division Robbie certainly wasn't one of them.

In view of his recent connection with Burnley, Robbie was in touch with some of the lads at the club and Steve told me that Robbie wanted to come back, and asked me if we should go in for him. All Burnley fans love Robbie and the way he plays the game, but I thought that there was a slight risk he would be past his best fairly soon. He was thirty-one and he wanted a three year contract which made me slightly nervous, although with the benefit of hindsight I wouldn't have been. Leeds wanted five hundred thousand for him so I said to Steve:

"If you can get him for two hundred and fifty thousand we'll have him, but we're not going to spend more than that. Who knows if he can do three years for us in the first team?"

Steve was very good at doing a deal within a financial target. He'd always try to do the transaction within the budgeted figure, and in this case it took a few weeks but by the end of July we signed Robbie on a three year deal for two hundred and fifty thousand. Everyone was happy.

Towards the end of summer, Turf Moor had hosted an England B international against Albania. Steve and I both admired Besart Berisha playing for the Albanians, probably because he scored their goal. But he looked very quick and skilful so when we talked about him after the game we both agreed that he might be worth a look.

The following week Steve made a few enquiries out in Hamburg where Besart was playing, and he watched him again. It looked like he could be a good inside forward or a winger so we put in an offer for him straight away and it went to tribunal.

I was aware that as a club we had consistently failed at tribunals where other clubs had succeeded and that bewildered me. I thought that we needed to be well prepared and get the best legal advisers because there must be a right way of doing it. So we decided to hire the Manchester United director Maurice Watkin's firm Brabners Chaffe Street. And the week before the tribunal date we put together a formal tribunal plan.

Our advisers did a lot of the preparation for us. They produced some DVDs and looked at Besart's international and domestic career, and we were ready with a really slick presentation. The tribunal was set in early August in a pretty grim hotel in Sheffield. Transfer tribunals are a bit like a court hearing with a panel of about ten judges, and on this occasion when we got there one or two of the judges hadn't arrived. Actually, Steve and I were there about an hour early. So we were ushered into a little room at the side to get ourselves a cup of tea.

We were helping ourselves to the tea when in walked Maurice Watkins and Sir Alex Ferguson. I thought, 'Wow what are they doing here?' It turned out that they weren't making a late swoop for Besart, but they were there for the hearing of Anderson, who United were signing for around twenty million. And they were due in after us. As we were early for our hearing we had the best part of an hour with Sir Alex in the waiting room.

He was just back from his holidays so he was in a relaxed mood and full of animated stories. For the first fifteen minutes or so I think Steve was a bit in awe of Sir Alex. He was being very careful with his words because clearly he didn't want to make a bad impression. So I made small talk about his holidays and about his coach, Mick Phelan, who is of course a Burnley lad. I asked him how he got into management and what he thought were his key skills. He told me:

"When I was a younger manager, after every match I used to watch videos of our games all Saturday night. I watched them up to ten times to try to find every single mistake we'd made so that I could help and educate the players."

Now that's attention to detail. Sir Alex has an obsession to get it right. He continued:

"And you need really good people at youth level looking out for the players you need. You have to have a long term strategy for the club."

All this was sinking in as I listened intently. He was quite happy to share his thoughts on how to get success, how it takes hard work, players with character and an energetic manager. Steve was listening too and he started to try to find some common ground between himself and Sir Alex. And I was hoping that he might hit on Sir Alex for a few players. Something like, 'How's about letting us have that Ronaldo for a year?'

Eventually the moment came when Steve made his move. He waited for a pause and then said:

"Wellbeck's a player."

Sir Alex looked up with a furrowed brow and replied quietly:

"Yes, he's got a career."

I sat there waiting for the follow up - but it didn't come. So we went back to talking about holidays.

Soon enough we went into the tribunal which was very much like a court hearing. The atmosphere was formal and we followed a laid out procedure whereby the history of the player was discussed before Steve had his opportunity to talk about the merits of the signing for both the player and the football club. He was being very careful with his words and presenting the case well for Besart to sign, and we then moved on to watch video clips of Besart in action which had been compiled by our lawyers.

But when we put the video on the opening thirty seconds were of a John Wayne movie! Initially I think people thought we were signing somebody from the Wild West. The hilarity around the room had just about subsided when the clips of football started. I think it may have been an advantage for us because it settled the atmosphere in the room and it probably helped us to get the signing done. Our slick presentation had clearly impressed!

Not long after that there was a Labour Party dinner and Steve had been invited to go along by Alastair Campbell. He spent a lot of the time at the bar with Sir Alex there and he clearly has a huge amount of respect for him. But in the meantime, having failed to secure a few players from United, we looked down the road to the City of Manchester Stadium to try to bolster our defence. John Harley wasn't a long term prospect for us at left back and we knew that Stephen Jordan had become available at Manchester City. He's a bigger lad and he was well regarded at City within the club and by the fans. I think he endeared himself to the City faithful when he kept Ronaldo in his pocket during a rare and famous victory for the sky blues. Initially Jordan wanted to go to Stoke but Steve met with him and his agent to see if he could persuade him to join us. But after the meeting there was no follow up from their side. Steve chased the agent a few times but didn't get a reply, which really annoyed him.

Then a week before the first game of the season the agent rang Steve to tell him that Jordan hadn't signed for anyone yet. In a major effort at controlling his natural inclinations, Steve said to me:

"I was going to tell him to get lost Bren; but you tell me that I shouldn't always say the things I'm thinking straight away. So I stopped, bit my lip, and said okay mate, okay mate we should talk."

So we signed Stephen Jordan to add to the pre-season squad. It hadn't been a bad summer's work. We'd brought in Robbie and Berisha up front, got a new left back and a goalkeeper. All in all we felt pretty positive as we went on our pre-season tour to Austria. I missed the tour because I was on a family holiday to the hidden city of Petra in Jordan. As we toured the city we decided to pay for a donkey ride to take us back up to our hotel. When we asked our guide for his name he said, 'Jesus' and I said to Ellen:

"Bloody Hell, here I am on a donkey with a man called Jesus. Maybe we are on the road to something special!"

6

Changing Of the Guard

August – November 2007

'Every man's work, whether it be literature or music or picture or architecture or anything else, is always a portrait of himself.' Samuel Butler

The afternoon before our first match of the new season felt like Christmas Eve. I just couldn't wait for it all to start again. And the great thing was that we had a chance to get going again in the Championship, when at times in the second half of the last season it looked like we might well be trying to work our way out of League One.

And we had been meticulous in our preparations. A lot of work had gone on in the summer, not only in getting a better squad of players together but also in trying to improve everything that we offered at the club. So on the Friday afternoon I made my way over to Burnley to ensure we were ready for the opening day. I was tremendously excited. I think every fan is excited the day before the new season. To get our sport fix we spend half the summer watching cricket matches getting rained off and the other half watching football DVDs. Every two years we get plenty of live international football, and we get mildly excited watching England. But in all honesty it isn't really all that important, not when you compare it to watching your own team, whether it's Burnley, Arsenal or Halifax Town.

When I arrived at the ground I went up into the back of the Longside, the James Hargreaves Stand to check the food kiosks and see that all the displays were up and ready. Our first fixture was an absolute cracker, at home to West Brom, the pre-season favourites, and we were hoping for a big attendance. Then my phone rang and it was Steve:

"Where are you?" He sounded kind of furtive and a little agitated.

"I'm here at the ground now," I replied.

"Meet me on the pitch in two minutes."

I wandered down and stepped onto the playing surface. It was a beautiful sunny day and the pitch looked like Wembley. That gave me a tingle. I've felt that buzz a thousand times when the Clarets run out onto the pitch; and no matter what's gone before, the first game of the season has that incredible sense of anticipation. Steve stood in the centre circle wearing his trademark white shorts and tight training top and with a cup of tea in his hand. As I walked over I could smell the grass and was still thinking about the game the following day. I was so excited about all the effort we had put in. Would it add up to anything? Maybe, maybe not.

Steve was looking a bit worried so I said:

"You alright?"

"No."

"What's the matter?" I asked.

"Effin' Wayne Thomas, that's what the matter is."

Sometimes you need a fairly broad mind when you're dealing with problems that footballers might cause, and it often pays not to hope for the best. As a centre back, Wayne could be pretty useful but I didn't know much about him as a man:

"Why, what's he done?"

"The sod wants a transfer!"

Not good. It would probably have been better if Steve had said, 'He's injured himself while been arrested for drunken and lewd behaviour at the Press Club'. Wayne had spent a fair bit of the previous season injured or suspended but he'd finished in great form. He'd done well to overcome a difficult start at the club and had become one of our most consistent players, and we all felt he could be a major presence this year. Steve told me that Southampton had made an offer so I told him not to worry because as far as the club was concerned Wayne wasn't going anywhere. But the manager wasn't convinced:

"Hmmm, it's not that simple Bren. He bloody well wants to go. He knows what money he'll get there. Southampton is a big club!"

That did put a slightly different light on things. Money is by no means always the main motivating factor for players but in some cases it can help to weaken the resolve. So I asked Steve what he thought. He was obviously worried that we'd struggle to hang on to Wayne for long:

"Well, we might be able to keep him for a week or two and see what happens, but I need to line someone else up in case."

We had already talked about David Unsworth because his contract at Wigan had expired. He'd been a top class defender for over a decade in the Premiership. He was obviously getting near to the end of his playing career but he could certainly plug a gap in our division. We knew he had spoken to Stoke as well but still hadn't agreed terms. So I said:

"Okay, let's invite him in and give him a one year deal."

Steve agreed but for the time being he was keen to play Wayne the day after. It would have been very difficult to leave him out and move things round at this late stage, and I knew that this was as big a game for Steve as it was for me. I sort of hoped that we had shelved Steve's immediate worry, albeit for only a few days and I wanted to make sure he was right up for the new season:

"How do you feel?" I asked.

"Okay, okay." He was tense as you'd expect just before such a big game. But I thought a reassurance wouldn't go amiss:

"Look Steve, I want you to know that all we want you to think about is fifth or sixth. If you get us into fifth or sixth that's top two for Burnley. Don't worry about any more than that. I'm certain it's possible that we can get there and we'll support you as much as we can."

I didn't want to put any more pressure on Steve, but I did want him to know my ambition for the team. He was still apprehensive:

"Expectations are higher now though Bren. You're here, we've bought a few players and the fans want glory now don't they?"

I couldn't argue with any of that, and in reality I didn't want to. As fans we all want glory every season:

"Well that's football isn't it? Just do your best and I'm sure that'll get us there Steve."

Steve was looking down at the pitch and I said:

"It's fantastic, the pitch, isn't it? I can't wait for the match tomorrow."

He looked around himself with some disdain, and to my astonishment said:

"It's shit!"

"What do you mean it's shit? Look it's absolutely beautiful."

"It's got all this wild grass in it." I couldn't see any. *"Look here, here and here."*

I still couldn't see any, and I couldn't see how Steve could see any so I said:

"I bet you're one of those blokes who has all his shirts lined up in whites, blues and greens and you have all your black suits together and all your other suits together."

Steve gave me a puzzled look and said:

"Have you been to my house?"

We both laughed and wished each other luck for the season.

There's no doubt about it he was a perfectionist at heart. Things that were slightly wrong would irritate him but I think they would bother him more than they probably should. There wasn't a lot I could do about the grass concern. It still looked magnificent to me so I went back to the beer counters.

♦

The morning of the first game was just as beautiful and sunny as the day before, and everything was set up for the big start. I was desperately keen that we would make a good impression, and with all the entertainment we'd planned to ensure that we had a carnival atmosphere, the weather was just perfect.

The pre-match entertainment was my agenda. I wanted to make sure that we gave value for money to the fans. Outside the ground we had a reggae band, face painting, stilt walkers and there was a fabulous mood of celebration about the place. I know that some of our more traditionalist supporters would prefer to have lower key, or preferably no entertainment. But you won't bring as many new families and younger fans in by offering a half hour wait with a cup of Bovril. In any case the traditionalists just care about what happens on the pitch and we all share in that aspiration.

And this was the first time that we played the fantastic half time, 'Pie and Chips' competition. It's our own version of Sky Sports Soccer AM's game, where groups of lads have a chance to chip as many footballs as they can through a hole in a big inflatable in two minutes. It seemed only right that our target should be a huge inflatable pie, as our shirt sponsor was Hollands Pies, although admittedly at first sight the hole made it look a bit like a giant donut. I thought it would be good fun to kick it off with a team made up of the directors of the club. So I recruited Barry, Martin Hobbs, John Turkington and Clive Holt. We needed seven so my youngest lad Conor and one of his mates joined in.

As we strolled towards the big inflatable pastry Barry and I quite fancied ourselves but we didn't hold out much hope for the others. Barry played for Burnley reserves in his youth so I was keen to see him in action. Clive Holt, who has been a director for 23 years, would be the first to admit that he's not the best at footy and I didn't really know how good Martin and John were. Clive actually borrowed the giant inflatable pie to be erected in his back garden during that week, and he had spent the whole week practising. I don't know how many he scored in the week but I suspect his greenhouse was in more danger.

So with the warm up music playing, Darren Bentley, our communications guy, chuckling down the microphone and the corner of the Bob Lord Stand looking on in bewilderment, Barry hit the rim of the pie with our first shot. I missed, John missed then up stepped Clive to hit a classic toe bunger broadly in the right direction, which unbelievably sailed through the middle of the pie. To our astonishment Clive had scored the first goal! Then Martin got one and before the two minutes were up the lads got one each. Barry and I had been well and truly humbled. As the season went on it turned out that four was actually a decent score and we finished up in the top six.

Apart from that it was a memorable day. I was thrilled to see a 16,000 crowd turn out to produce a great atmosphere and we ended up beating Tony Mowbray's league favourites 2-1. I saw Steve after the game and we both felt confident about the whole day. I knew I'd speak to him in the morning after we'd both watched 'The Championship' on ITV. Sure enough at eleven Steve was on the phone because Palace had battered Southampton 4-1 on the opening day and he said:

"George Burley's been on and he's offered us six hundred thousand for Wayne."

"Just say 'no'." We needed to be resolute on this.

"Okay Bren, what if they come back higher?"

"Just say, 'no'. We need him don't we? He's part of our plans."

I had a suspicion that wouldn't be the end of it and less than an hour later Steve was on again:

"Bren, they might go up to seven fifty."

I was standing firm on this:

"Well we're not interested are we Steve? We've got our own plans and we need Wayne Thomas."

But Southampton were playing at Peterborough in the Carling Cup live on TV on the Monday and Steve said:

"If they get beat there they'll be on again. What shall I say?"

We had signed David Unsworth as cover, but then Steve Caldwell had been injured on the first day. But every player has his price so I suggested that if Southampton offered a million for Wayne we'd have to do it, because arguably he wasn't worth a million to us. We agreed to talk again and to make a decision on Monday night.

Sure enough Peterborough beat Southampton and within five minutes of the game finishing Steve was on the phone again:

"They'll be on again tomorrow."

"Well you know what to do. If they offer one million we'll do it and then you need to start thinking about who we can sign to replace him."

Predictably, the following day George Burley reluctantly offered one million for Wayne and we agreed to sell him. Steve then needed to find a good replacement before the end of the week. All credit to Steve, he made a few quick phone calls and in the afternoon rang me to say:

"What would you give for Clark Carlisle?"

I've always been an admirer of Clark Carlisle having seen him at Blackpool and QPR, and then he was at Watford when they were promoted to the Premier League. He even stood out when he was on loan at Luton in the drab 0-0 draw at Turf Moor a few months earlier. So I answered Steve's question:

"Clark Carlisle has got to be worth between three fifty and four hundred thousand."

"What If I said we could get him for two fifty?"

"Bargain, make an offer and let's have him."

We discussed his obvious qualities as a real presence on the pitch, a natural winner and leader.

So Steve called Adie Boothroyd at Watford and we agreed the fee that afternoon.

But on the Wednesday the two of us were on tenterhooks. Wayne Thomas was on his way to Southampton for his fitness test, and he'd been injury prone during the previous twelve months. At the same time Clark Carlisle was preparing to head up the M1 to sign for us. We didn't want to sign Clark unless Wayne had passed his medical which was on that afternoon, so we rang Clark to tell him to come up on the Thursday, by which time we'd have Wayne's results. Timing in football is everything. We had the chance to get a million for Wayne and then buy Clark for a quarter of that.

Then at lunchtime on the Thursday Steve rang me:

"Guess what. Wayne's passed his medical and he's signed for Southampton. He's a Saints player."

Fantastic! Clark was due in an hour and he signed straight away, in time for our second match away at Scunthorpe. A lot of people had a double take when the news came through that we had signed Clark Carlisle for two hundred and fifty thousand and got a million for Wayne Thomas. Most people thought the figures had been quoted the wrong way round! It was an outstanding piece of business for the club and both Steve and I were absolutely delighted. I was really pleased with Steve because he had negotiated two quick deals here brilliantly, and it really was good business.

And Steve hadn't finished his astute run of clever business. We became aware that up the road at Preston their influential right back Graham Alexander was unhappy that his club hadn't offered him an extension to his contract. He was a legend at Deepdale, having been there for over ten years and been involved in several play-off campaigns. When the opportunity came to sign Graham, Steve was very quick to spot that he would be another ideal leader within our team. Clearly there was a gamble on Graham's age, he was already 35, but anyone who knows him sees that he is a consummate professional and he's as eager to play as any eighteen year old.

And when Steve rang me, I had a mental vision of the goals that Graham had put past us and I knew that he was an iconic figure in Preston. It was too good an opportunity for us to miss. Steve made an opportunistic swoop on our neighbours which cost us £250,000. At the time some of our supporters regarded the move as an unnecessary risk, but it was a measured risk that was mitigated by Graham's subsequent performance as the magnificent player and leader he is. He has repaid our faith in him innumerable times.

Steve deserves a lot of credit for bringing in those players at the start of the season.

♦

As I became more involved at the club some of the directors started to introduce me to some of their business activities. John Sullivan has always had an active interest in the Duke of Edinburgh Award. When John asked me to support the charity I was happy to get involved. The Duke of Edinburgh Award Scheme actively encourages young people to work towards a goal and improve themselves, and if they are successful they might get the opportunity to visit Buckingham Palace.

As a result of my involvement I was invited down to Buckingham Palace myself to have lunch with a group of sponsors to meet with Prince Edward. I arrived at the Palace at about five minutes to twelve to be greeted by a huge crowd of spectators outside the gates preparing to watch the Changing of the Guard. I was trying to work out how to get in and after realising there wasn't a side entrance I went back to the main gates and said to the sentry:

"Excuse me; I need to get in because I've been invited to lunch by Prince Edward."

He asked me for ID but all I could produce was my Barclaycard. Much to my relief the sentry looked me up and down, checked his list, took a lingering view of my Barclaycard and I was in. All this coincided with the changing of the guard, so as I made my way towards the front door of Buckingham Palace I noticed the guards were marching from the opposite direction, and at the speed I was going they would catch up with me about ten yards short of the front door! So in front of several thousand tourists I started a sprint walk in an attempt to avoid interrupting the Queens parade.

They must have been watching me from inside the Palace because as I hurried towards the front door, before I could knock on the door it opened. Fortunately my momentum didn't make me fall inside! I was met by five secret service types who again looked me up and down, and feeling nervous of the situation I made my excuses for my unfortunate lack of ID.

After a brief group introduction downstairs we were then taken upstairs to the main room on the first floor. As I walked up the stairs towards the dining room I was taking in the amazing experience. The walls displayed enormous paintings of past monarchs and battles from centuries gone by. I was totally in awe of the occasion.

In the dining room there was standing room only. Prince Edward made a short speech and we were invited to have a drink. I got myself an orange juice because I was afraid of making an inappropriate joke. I then picked up a plate of food, and was just figuring out how to eat and drink, as there was nowhere to put my glass down, when Prince Edward walked over to me with his hand outstretched. I managed to pass my glass to the chap standing next to me in time to shake the Prince's hand, before engaging nervously in conversation for fifteen minutes. I'm sure I must have inspired him to discuss Burnley over dinner with Prince Charles! Prince Charles has a warm affection for the town and is taking an active part in the Weavers Triangle project.

♦

The following week I was in my office at work when I had a call from my daughter Sinead. She rang to tell me that Ellen wasn't well and had called for an ambulance. This was really worrying because Ellen's a tough cookie so I thought that it must be something serious. She'd had a stomach pain which we thought might be a touch of food poisoning she picked up on holiday. But when she was admitted to hospital it turned out that she had internal haemorrhaging. And frighteningly the consultant thought there was a risk it might be cancerous, which was later cleared thankfully.

The next couple of months were pure chaos. I was very worried about Ellen and it was also a time when I knew the business world was changing. I could see that the corporate landscape was shifting rapidly and it was concerning me, but at the same time I was getting pulled away from the front line. And to make matters worse, at the time Ellen fell ill John Davies, my finance director, got a trapped nerve in his back and he was in agony. He couldn't sleep and was off work for a month. John never takes time off and if Ellen was my right arm, then John was my left.

Before all this had happened in early 2007, I had talked to John about laying off some risk on the development side. We had decided that we should sell off twenty per cent of the development business, Modus Ventures, to get some capital into the business to reduce our short term debt. I knew it was the right time for us to bring in a large institutional shareholder. So straight after the summer holidays we pulled together a data room, and prepared to go out to the market with a proposal. But with Ellen's illness and John's absence, the plan was delayed; and I knew it was a time lapse that could cause problems. Eventually, by the autumn we had put the package out to several banks, all of which knew us well. RBS introduced their private equity arm who made an offer of thirty million cash in for twenty per cent of the development business. They started their due diligence in December but initially I had hoped that the deal would have been done by October. By January 2008 it was becoming known to customers that there was a growing problem with the banks, and in February the deal was pulled. We thought we had thirty million on the way for twenty percent and as quickly as it was there it was gone. It was a worrying moment. If I'd got the transaction done before Christmas we'd have been home and dry.

So amidst the chaos of September and October the football was actually quite a nice diversion. I was still committing the same amount of time to the club and increasing my investment. So far I'd committed four million pounds in 2006/07 and had legally contracted to invest another two million that season and I managed to stay in constant dialogue with Steve. Barry seemed content to sit back as I was funding the club and decisions were made quickly. I certainly felt able to determine the club's direction that season, and it was a frightening but exciting responsibility.

♦

I had recently been introduced to Alastair Campbell through the football club. He's an exceptional ambassador for Burnley and you can see his enthusiasm as a fan during every game that he attends, in his blog, and often when he appears on TV. I asked Alastair if he would do a lunch for me here at Modus with about fifty guests and during the evening we would hold a dinner for a broader network of businessmen. When he arrived at my offices I took him round to meet some of my staff, one of whom was Peter Macfarlane, who, as a Belfast boy, has a mind full of good conspiracy theories. I introduced him to Alastair and then I said:

"Pete, what's the latest conspiracy theory you're working on?

Pete shuffled from side to side and then he looked Alastair in the eye and said:

"Well Alastair, have you ever seen George Bush and Osama Bin Laden in the same room at the same time."

Alastair appeared somewhat surprised, so Pete went on:

"No you haven't. That's because they're the same man! The Bin Laden family were flown out of New York within two hours of 9/11 so there's got to be something in it."

Alastair enjoyed the theory but I'm not sure if he's explored it further since.

The dinner in the evening was at a hotel down in Cheshire and there were about eighty people in attendance. Alastair did a very enlightening speech about his career in politics, including the formation of New Labour. We ended the dinner with a question and answer session and after a fairly gentle start, one guest challenged some of the fundamental beliefs of the Labour Party. Alastair's retort was very strong and erudite, as you would expect, but the question had clearly got him into political mode and he responded very assertively to the next two or three follow up questions, at which point, I was beginning to shrivel down and hide in my seat. Thankfully the subject matter of the questions moved on to family and sport including his love of Burnley.

As the dinner came to an end I went over to Alastair and said:

"Thank you very much for coming up for the day Alastair; we've really enjoyed what you've said it was fascinating." Then I paused before I ventured:

"A couple of the questions there got you a little bit energised."

Alastair's eyes narrowed as he turned to me and said:

"I really hate Tories!"

◆

As the season got going we beat Oldham 3-0 in the Carling Cup on a Tuesday night. It was a good result but Oldham could have had a hatful and the only difference between the two sides was our finishing. The following week we had a disappointing home draw with Blackpool and then we had a bit of a sticky spell. We won our next match at Sheffield Wednesday, but they were dreadful, having lost their first six games and they visibly had no confidence. I'd have backed North End to get a result that night. Bayern that is, not Preston.

Then we went on a run of nine games with only one win, a home result against Norwich who are often as kind to us as Plymouth. As the poor run gathered pace Steve was getting more and more agitated. Slightly bizarrely, in my opinion, he was expressing regret that we'd sold Wayne Thomas.

Steve and I had built up a friendship over the previous ten months or so and he was quite open with me. When Sammy Lee was fired at Bolton and Chris Hutchins at Wigan, he hinted to me that maybe he should try his luck and go for jobs there. I knew that he had made a couple of strategic phone calls to Wigan and Bolton. And he had actually asked Sir Alex to give him a reference for the Wigan job, so I was concerned that he was far from settled. He was feeling under more pressure at Burnley and was acutely conscious of what had happened during the nineteen game run in the previous season, when we hadn't dismissed him. But this spell certainly wasn't good. We'd spent a lot of money by Burnley's standards and brought in nine or ten players since I'd been at the club but I could see that he was becoming more aggravated and impatient with the players. You could see it during matches on the touchline.

And Steve had started commenting that Burnley was a small club. I don't think he felt he was getting the rewards for all the effort he had put in, even though he was fairly well paid. And to make matters worse there was a growing tension between Steve and one or two directors on the board. In his conversations with me he referred to his growing frustration with 'the energy sappers on the board.' And after a 3-2 home defeat by Southampton he came into the chairman's lounge after the game, clearly angry and swearing. He was venting his spleen quite spectacularly about the players, the club and everyone who was at fault apart from himself.

Going back to my general philosophy that I always give people twelve months to prove themselves, I started to review our progress and what we had achieved in that time. And I have to admit that I was concerned that we might have wasted some of the financial investment. Steve was still asking me if we could go in for more players, like Darren Huckerby at Norwich and Lee Bromby at Sheffield United. I felt that they were older players who wouldn't add anything to the club; and we'd be laying out a lot more cash for very little benefit. The difference in our views about the sort of players we should be signing was widening at this point. And Steve was becoming concerned that by October I no longer supported him, and he wanted more players.

Then on a miserable night on the 6th November we played Hull City at home. They were near the bottom of the division and a team that we should beat if we were well organised. Ellen and the whole family came along and we invited some friends who were Hull fans. It was a cold night and a desperately poor crowd of about 9,900. The atmosphere was terrible and it was obvious that a lot of people were beginning to feel the recurring pain of the nineteen games without a win from the previous season, and fans were starting to question what we were doing. But most of the fans didn't know that Steve had already expressed that he didn't believe he had long left at Burnley and, naturally for an ambitious man, he had one eye on a Premiership job.

The game was absolutely dire from start to finish and Steve was getting some criticism from a section of fans in the Bob Lord Stand. The supporters were becoming as impatient as he was and they had every right to be. At the start of the season I thought we had a reasonable chance of making it to the top six. But three months into the season it was obvious that we still weren't good enough overall.

We lost the game 1-0 and I was completely horrified. It was such a bad performance that we had been outplayed by Hull. At the time we had no idea that they'd end up being promoted and they just looked like a workmanlike Hull team. This was a real milestone. Bloody hell we'd just been outclassed by Hull!

The next morning I woke up at five 'o clock. I usually sleep very well and I only struggle if I have something big on my mind. As I got up I said to Ellen:

"I think we need a new manager."

I went down into the kitchen, made a coffee and started putting together a list of people we'd consider if Steve wasn't our manager. And as soon as it was a decent hour I rang Barry and told him that I was convinced that we needed a change:

"Barry I think we should take the bull by the horns. If we change now we'll probably have more choice, but if we wait until January there might be fewer decent managers available. If we open up the running now we might get some good candidates and it allows a new manager the chance to recruit a few players in January."

We shared our concerns over the club's current difficulties and agreed that I should meet with Steve.

Steve and I always exchanged phone calls the day after a game, and he had rung me twice on the Wednesday afternoon but I hadn't taken the calls because I was still annoyed. At about four pm and at the third time of ringing I answered the call:

"Hi Steve."

"Okay." He paused, sensing a problem. *"How are you mate?"*

"Well, not good. It was shit last night."

Over the past year we'd got to know each other pretty well and Steve could read me, certainly on this occasion:

"Yep, it was. Have you got something to say Bren?"

It almost had the emotional awkwardness of two twenty year olds splitting up after a bumpy twelve month relationship but my language was a bit more detached:

"Yeah, it's time for a change Steve."

Even though I think in his heart he knew it may have been coming he was a bit taken aback and I could tell that he was understandably upset. So I said to him:

"Look, why don't you come round tonight for dinner and we'll talk it through. I'm sorry Steve."

Then I rang Ellen and said:

"Can you rustle something up? I've got Steve Cotterill coming round and it's not going to be the best evening."

This clearly presented Ellen with a bit of a dilemma:

"What do you do for an evening like that?" And she started talking about the type of food you should do when you're changing the manager! *"Do you want beers or do you not want beers?"*

When Steve arrived he was dropped off by a driver so I think he was expecting a few drinks. He later described the meal as the 'Last Supper' and I don't think he was referring to the fish! As we sat talking he was quite upset and I was genuinely moved. He'd put a lot of effort in over the past few years and he'd done a good job for the club, but I explained to him that I didn't think he could take us up and we needed a different style to make things happen. And maybe it would be better if he tried to focus on going for jobs in the Premiership, because I knew he wanted to.

So we agreed that he'd leave by mutual consent. At that moment it was the best thing for Steve and for the club. It was one of the most difficult days I have ever experienced and it genuinely scared me that I was then responsible for changing Burnley's manager. I actually expected Steve to walk into the manager's job at Wigan or possibly Preston shortly thereafter but it didn't happen for him.

♦

The following morning I was on the seven 'o clock train from Manchester to Euston when I rang Barry. I had my hand over my phone as I explained to Barry what had happened and that Steve had taken it well, all things considered.   Barry was in Germany that day so we agreed we'd do the press conference on the Friday.

As I sat in my meeting later that morning my phone started ringing non stop. And when I went outside to look at my messages they were from the newspapers and Sky Sports. Steve had gone into training in the morning and told the players, who true to form texted their agents and off it went into the ether. And in a further bizarre twist it turned out that my hushed conversation with Barry had been picked up by a Burnley fan sat opposite me on the train and then downloaded onto the Clarets Mad website. I couldn't believe it.

So we had a hurriedly arranged press conference back at the club on the Thursday afternoon. I met Steve before the press arrived and he went over a couple of points on his contract. He's always been a strong negotiator and that had served the club well, and he left with a healthy compensation package.

Looking back that Friday, I was convinced that we'd done the right thing. After all, we had been sliding down the league. We couldn't afford to have another winless run of matches and we had to do better. But the next two weeks were daunting. Without doubt they are on the shortlist for the worst weeks of my life. I had people ringing me all the time and you can't help watching Sky Sports and listening to comments when the topic is discussed on the radio. There were phone-ins on Radio Lancashire with guys ringing up and saying, 'I don't think we should have got rid of Steve Cotterill so quickly' and 'it's obviously Flood who's sacked him.' The consensus was pretty much fifty-fifty and for the half who supported Steve it was clear that whoever was brought in would be 'Flood's man'.

I knew that whatever we decided to do here would be make or break in terms of what the Burnley public thought of me. I had joined the board merely as an enthusiastic fan with the sole objective of trying to get us promoted, but I wasn't sure I was ready for this level of responsibility.

Treasured photo of Teresa and Duncan

Me with Dad and Steve

Winning the Estates Gazette Award

Brunshaw Celtic

Me and Barry with Steve at his leaving press conference

Modus team on It's a Knockout

Sinead, Kevin, Conor and Ellen

Me and Barry welcome Owen to Turf Moor

Beast saves and puts Chelsea out!

(back row) Mr Hollands Pie, John Turkington, Clive Holt,
Martin Hobbs, Barry, Me, Bertie Bee
(front row) George Greenhalgh, Charlie Greenhalgh, Conor Flood

37,000 Clarets at Wembley

My good friend Steve Tattersall and me with
our two boys who were mascots at Wembley

Ellen and Me before Kick off at Wembley

Wade Elliot's promotion winning goal at Wembley

Champagne on the pitch

Champions

7

Da Da Da Da Da ....Owen Coyle

November 2007

'Never underestimate the other guy.' Jack Welch

The ending of Steve's era at Turf Moor was without doubt the hardest thing I'd had to do since I arrived at the club barely twelve months earlier. But it was done, and having made that decision, we now had to figure out how we could get somebody to make a difference. We were determined to find somebody who was capable of taking us up to the Premiership.

I was acutely aware that I didn't have the unequivocal support of the town at this time. I had picked up very early in the process that the consensus in Burnley was, quite rightly, that I was being judged for this decision. As you can imagine I now felt an immense pressure to make sure that we got the next appointment absolutely right.

When I first joined the board at Burnley I had decided to get some guidance from figureheads who were successful and experienced in the game, so I went to see Dave Whelan at Wigan to pick his brains. Dave's quite sensible with his money, which I guess is partly why he is so successful. So much so that when we went for lunch he even went to the extent of ordering tap water to drink. I thought he was winding me up, but he wasn't! I took the chance to ask Dave for his advice on buying players, which agents we should use and which we should steer clear of. After he'd sat back and thought about it for a moment he said:

"You know Brendan; it's all down to the manager. If you make the right decision on the manager you'll do well. If you make the wrong decision you'll do badly. It's as simple as that."

The clarity of Dave's words had stuck with me and as we were now in that very position, they had become more relevant than ever.

Throughout the next couple of weeks there was a hotline to my mobile from the press. Radio Lancashire, Suzanne Geldard and Chris Boden were on the phone almost every day.

As the furore seemed to gather pace, I knew that the best thing to do was to get on with the job in hand quickly. So Barry and I got to work agreeing the criteria that we were looking for in our next manager, and this is what we came up with:

- We need someone who is familiar with Burnley or a very similar club.
- They need to have good knowledge of the Championship.
- They must have a good track record.
- Someone with modern coaching skills.
- Someone who was passionate about the academy.
- And has the ability and network to bring in promising young players, who could join the first team squad immediately.

We also agreed that we would prefer a young manager if possible, but this wasn't an immovable prerequisite.

These criteria were essential for us to be able to find the right man and gave us a fairly vivid profile, so it didn't look like finding our man would be an easy job. But there was no way that we were willing to settle for second best. We simply had to get the right man. But the criteria we had set didn't seem to narrow down the field much. We were bombarded from all sorts of avenues and I began to make a detailed list to add to the one I'd started on the morning after the 'Last Supper'. The sort of names that were cropping up were Gary Speed, Mike Newall, Peter Reid, Billy Davies, Nigel Worthington and Paul Jewell; and I made a note of every contact we received. Well to be honest not every single one. You do get the full range of applicants coming at you and for some reason we seemed to get our fair share of the odd ones. One day when I was at the club Barry handed this one to me, and he wandered off without another word, but I was unaware that his shoulders were shaking:

To: Chairman
Cc: FA

Dear Mr Kilby

I would like to apply for the post of, 'Manager of Burnley Football Club'.

I have 5 years experience of being a Manager in the 'Fantasy League'. In the five years that I've been manager I have taken Real Barca to the top of the Premier league. In my first year we were runners up; in my second year we won the title and qualified for Champions League Football.

I'm used to working with a budget of £40,000,000, but I do realise I will not be getting that kind of money at Turf Moor.

I come from a footballing background; I was captain of my school team all through my school years. We won the league one year and got to the cup final which unfortunately we lost.

I played for East Area Boys and had a trial for Manchester Boys at which I was told I would have progressed had I not scored two own goals. I am also close friends with soccer guru, John Stanhope, who used to manage Manchester City Women's team.

There will be no problem with relocation because I live close by in Accrington. Please contact me as soon as possible as I have heard through the grapevine that Real Madrid may be on the lookout for a new manager too.

Yours Sincerely

Steven Ounce

I did have a plan to ring every applicant personally, which I immediately scrapped. And so we set to work in narrowing the list down a bit. We were nearer the mark with the likes of Sammy McIlroy who was doing a solid job at Morecambe, and Simon Grayson, who had worked wonders at Blackpool with very little resource.

Mick Phelan was an obvious name that came to mind. He's a Burnley lad and still lives in the area. He still comes to matches when he can and he's got a fantastic pedigree having worked for Sir Alex for so long. I rang Mick but he didn't return my call.

♦

My personal favourite was Brian Laws. He'd been an outstanding player for Burnley and like a lot of our ex-players was still very fond of the club and our supporters. And he had done his time in management, having completed a successful shift at Scunthorpe and moving up to Sheffield Wednesday where, in his first full year in charge, he had a very good win ratio of 44 per cent. But one of our directors warned me off him because of a little fracas he was involved with when he was manager at Grimsby Town. Brian spent just under two years as manager there, but apparently his relationship took a turn for the worse when, during an argument on a night out, he allegedly threw a chicken wing at his Italian winger Ivano Bonetti, which hit the player in the face, and then a full on scrap ensued! The alleged incident took place in a Kentucky Fried Chicken restaurant and consequently Brian was given the nickname, 'The Colonel' which followed him to Hillsborough.

So ignoring my co-director's advice I made a direct approach to Sheffield Wednesday and asked for their permission to speak to Brian. Wednesday still weren't playing particularly well but they turned down our approach. Obviously we wouldn't speak to the manager directly in a case like this, but I did find out that Brian would have loved to have come to Burnley and he wasn't best pleased with the board at Hillsborough to say the least. The owners he didn't like there at the time have gone now, but I'm sure that he would have relished the job at Burnley at that time.

So we turned our attention to the other candidates. We thought about Mike Newall, who had caught our eye because of the good style of football they had played at Luton. But his Blackburn connection might have worked against us. You can't afford to be too parochial, but on the other hand you can't be absolutely sure that an ex-Blackburn player will end up having a love affair with the Longsiders at Burnley.

When we had parted company with Steve Cotterill, he had recommended Joe Royle to me as he thought we'd struggle to do better. I thanked Steve because I knew how he admired Joe, but he didn't really get near to fitting our brief.

By the end of the week I had spoken to all of the serious candidates on the phone and we were getting close to a shortlist made up of Paul Jewell, Peter Reid and our own Steve Davis, who was assistant coach under Steve Cotterill and a legend with our fans.

Then out of the blue the club received an email from a journalist in Scotland, Alan Nixon, who said that Owen

Coyle might be interested in the job. Alan was a friend of his but I didn't know who Owen Coyle was. He wasn't on my first or second list and when I found out he was at St Johnstone I decided it wasn't really worth following up. I thought that it would be difficult to justify the decision if things went wrong after we had appointed a candidate from outside the mainstream. So I didn't give it any more thought. Barry and I agreed that we needed someone with a good standing in the game; someone who has either played for Burnley or who has a safe reputation.

That evening as I sat in my kitchen I was running through the names again – Steve Davis, Peter Reid, Paul Jewell - and then I looked at some of the others - Simon Grayson, John Gregory and Steve Staunton. I began to wonder if we had enough good candidates on the list or whether we'd need to go back to the drawing board. I was starting to feel the pressure of the decision and it was making me unusually nervous. It's not quite like making a decision for Modus. When I do that I do it for the good of the business, it might make us money and it might lose us money. But whatever the decision is, it isn't publicly aired, ready to be slated by forty thousand people who have every right to do so because it affects their lives in some way or another.

The more I looked at the list, the more I felt obliged to research each candidate thoroughly. So I thought I'd better ring Owen Coyle, the St Johnstone manager. His name was vaguely familiar to me but I couldn't remember who he'd played for. He'd been at Bolton probably around the time I was watching QPR and Arsenal in London, so obviously my football knowledge of the time had been dulled somewhat.

I rang Owen at about ten-thirty in the evening. I just felt that I needed to leave no stone unturned and through the week I had spoken to everyone with half a chance just to be clear in my own mind. I got Owen's answer-phone so left him a message and he rang back at about eleven. We were on the phone for about an hour as I went through the interview form that I'd prepared to ensure the questions I was asking each candidate were consistent. He had a fairly broad Glasgow accent and I found myself saying, 'pardon' a few times but I started to get a feel for the type of man he was and how he operated. I began by asking how he went about getting the best out of his players and I was quite impressed by how his reply developed:

"I think I've got good people skills. I'm very happy to make decisions at the football club and communicate them to the players. I always tell them early if they're going to be left out of the team."

He told me that he was at peak fitness and that he occasionally turned out for his team:

"I want the players to be the same as me. I want them to be the best that they possibly can be."

That really struck a chord for me. Owen went on:

"I want to get every ounce of effort from my players and I want them to be up front and honest. I make sure that they have respect for me and I have a huge amount of belief in them. They have a real 'day at work' attitude and a strong sense of community."

He told me that he felt it was vital to be there on the training ground every day but that, during the week, Sandy Stewart, his number two, often spoke to the players to avoid them hearing the same voice all the time. So far so good. So I asked Owen what he knew about the English game and he told me that he came down every week to watch a reserve game. And he continued:

"If I worked in England I'd have to be very selective in sourcing players from Scotland. But there's a player at Dundee United and one at Hearts that I'd want to bring down. They're good enough to play at Championship level. And I know that Ireland is a real hotbed of young talent."

It appealed to me that it looked like Owen would be able to source players from lower cost areas such as Scotland and Ireland, and within twenty minutes of speaking to him I was glad that I had. I was starting to think that this was a man who's not a million miles away from what we were looking for. He hadn't said anything that had worried me so far, so I asked him what his views on the youth academy were and he answered:

"It's so important Brendan. Eight out of my first team at St Johnstone are twenty-two or under, you've got to have young legs in your side. I'd want to get younger players into your football club, getting younger players in always revitalises the rest of the squad."

Owen had worked with strong role models like Bruce Rioch and Alex Mcleish and had also spent some time with Jack Charlton in Ireland. He had great admiration for Jack and spoke passionately about the simplicity of the big man's philosophy:

"I learned a lot from Jack. Players need to have a sense of spirit and a sense of community and from a leadership point of view that's absolutely vital at the football club. And home games are so important. We have an obligation to entertain our fans."

And that hit me right between the eyes. That obligation has been loud and clear at Burnley for most of our history but I hadn't felt entertained for a few years. Owen was getting on a roll now:

"I love to attack when we're at home. We've only lost two home games in the last two and a half years at Saints."

Owen had certainly struck a chord. We'd lost two home games in the last two and a half weeks at Turf Moor and I'm certain I'd have been more entertained at Burnley bus station. So I asked:

"How keen are you to come and work here in England Owen?

"Brendan, I'd do absolutely anything to work in England at that level. I'd come and do it for nothing!"

As we said goodbye I felt that Owen had definitely got his name on the list. He'd made a big impression on me. But I was still concerned about the nature of the gamble. He still wasn't quite proven enough and he didn't have a connection with Burnley, so all of that remained an issue. Everything he had said to me made me think that he would do everything in his power to be successful if he was given the chance. And when I looked at his record on Wikipedia, that strengthened his case as well. Anything over forty per cent is a good win ratio for a manager. Both Paul Jewell and Peter Reid were in the early forties. And although he'd only been a manager for three years, Owen was up at fifty per cent. In my own mind we now had a shortlist of four.

♦

The following morning I spoke with Barry and I told him that I'd had a conversation with Owen and I thought it had gone really well. But Barry wasn't easily convinced, mainly because Owen was from St Johnstone and he asked me what I thought of him:

"Well, he sounded a bit like Bill Shankly. Do you remember how Bill Shankly was?"

As it turned out Owen came from the same part of Glasgow as the great Shankly. I only hoped he might be touched with the same kind of genius.

"He's a strong family guy, three kids, a good catholic and he's teetotal."

That'd make a change for Burnley. And I could certainly relate to Owen's family background. I told Barry how his philosophy and work ethic had really made an impression on me, but he still wasn't sure:

"But he's from St Johnstone Brendan. He's an unknown entity."

That looked like it was going to be a sticking point for everyone. Not that St Johnstone is a poor club, quite the contrary, and Owen obviously had some success building up there. The year before they'd hit the Scottish national press by beating Rangers at Ibrox in the quarter final of the League Cup. And their recent record was excellent. But with the best will in the world, the Scottish League One isn't the Championship, and St Johnstone isn't Wolverhampton Wanderers.

But later that morning a slightly odd thing happened. I received a text from Phil Gartside, the chairman at Bolton Wanderers. It read:

"Hi Brendan – don't know if you're fixed up but have you had a look at Owen Coyle?"

I wondered what was going on so I rang Phil and asked:

"What do you know about Owen Coyle?"

Phil knew Owen well from his playing days and it turns out that Bolton actually considered him to replace Sammy Lee before they appointed Gary Megson earlier in the season. Now Phil's quite a measured thinker so it gave me some more encouragement that he thought so highly of Owen. So as soon as I'd spoken to Phil I rang Barry and asked him if he would be happy to meet Owen. And as luck would have it Barry was on his way up to Gleneagles for a romantic weekend with his partner Sonya, so he agreed to meet him for breakfast on the Saturday morning.

I wanted further evidence of his desire to get the job, so Owen had offered a reference from Alex McLeish, the Scotland manager, who was preparing the national team for a massive game against Italy on that Friday. I really didn't expect Alex to ring but, sure enough, within half an hour Alex was on the phone and he said:

"Brendan, Owen's a great fella; full of passion for the game and I have no doubt he will be a great success in the Championship. And I'm sure he'll be a Premiership manager one day."

I thanked Alex and I felt stronger again to push Owen on to the shortlist.

That Saturday, while Barry was meeting Owen, I was having breakfast with Paul Jewell. Paul had flagged up his interest in the job after someone in his family had heard me talking about it on the radio. I'd agreed with Barry that following our respective meetings we'd compare notes at lunchtime.

I was interested to know why Paul hadn't gone back to Wigan when Chris Hutchins had left a few weeks earlier and he replied:

"The players up there are on thirty, forty thousand a week and they're not interested. If I went in I would have to come down hard on the players." Then he added: *"And I got into a bit of social when I was there last time."*

Initially I wasn't sure what Paul meant by that but the tabloids later printed allegations of an affair. We got to discussing money at which point Paul was at pains to say that he wanted total control of team affairs and he would need three to four million to spend in the first transfer window. So that was a 'no' then. I agreed that we'd ring Paul again on the Monday. Paul had a few other opportunities and we agreed that Burnley wasn't at the top of his list.

Before I rang Barry I decided to take my dog for a walk, and while I was out Owen was on the phone, and he sounded pretty chirpy:

"Hi Brendan, I think I've had a good meeting with Barry and I liked what he said about the football club."

Owen had enjoyed the breakfast and now he was even keener to move things on, so he asked what the next step was. I said:

"Barry and I need to discuss it further and we'll get back to you in the next twenty four hours and we'll take it from there."

When I rang off I noticed that the last two digits on Owen's phone number are 18. This may sound a little strange but I am mildly superstitious and, believe it or not, my lucky number is 18. Not that this totally affected my judgement but it did help again. I do believe in fate. Now I realise that this revelation may send a lot of sensible, down to earth Clarets fans into a panic, frantically looking at all the donkeys in the football league who happen to be wearing the number 18. But please rest assured, I do try to keep my superstitious nature in check when I'm making decisions.

And in any case when I spoke to Barry at lunchtime he had been very impressed by Owen too. He felt that he was a genuine guy with a lot of integrity, but Barry was still clearly nervous of the St Johnstone status and his relatively short track record. But we were both becoming convinced that Owen was now a strong candidate in a field of four, and in all honesty I didn't think Paul Jewell was the man for us. We decided we'd ask him to do a short interview on Monday and we'd also speak to Peter Reid and Steve Davis so that we could make a decision that day, as time was moving on. Steve hadn't done himself any harm at all because he'd looked after the team the week before at Leicester where we had won 1-0. This Saturday we didn't have a game because it was an international weekend, but we needed our manager in place in time for the visit of Stoke, who were on a good run and were towards the top of the league, next Saturday.

♦

Peter Reid was the first on our interview list and he arrived at my offices in Manchester at nine on the Monday morning. As I approached him I noticed that he hadn't shaved and it did look like he'd had a bit of a late night. We sat down with a coffee and then Peter put this piece of paper that he'd been holding on the table. And then he nervously started his pitch in his hackneyed gruff Liverpool accent:

"I think I'll .... er .... you know, if I get the job .... I've been learning a bit about this sports science stuff

with Big Sam at Bolton. It's good like .... It's the way forward .... I've got some notes on it."

He looked at his piece of paper before gamely cracking on to play his trump card:

"And I went on a course with that Sir Clive Woodward. I've learnt some things on that as well and I could do some of that."

I looked at Barry and I was thinking, 'has he just pulled this together this morning?' Barry was looking somewhat bemused too. So we asked him a few more questions. There's no doubt that Peter's a likeable guy. He's got a great sense of humour but Barry and I were concerned that he'd had a couple of years out of the game and he might not be hungry enough for us. But his record speaks for itself and we thought that maybe he would come back into the game refreshed. And one thing that was in his favour was that he would bring Adrian Heath in as his right arm man. Adrian had been popular here in his time as a player and manager, and the Burnley factor is always a consideration. Then Peter started to chat about what his style would be and who he'd source his players from:

"I'm pals with Sir Alex, and I could get that kid Jonny Evans. And there's this great centre forward at Vauxhall Motors."

I didn't try too hard to hide my surprise:

"Vauxhall Motors?"

"Yeah, yeah, yeah .... He's playing there because he's been a bit of a bad lad like. He's been in prison for three years!"

After he'd gone we moved on to Paul Jewell, who we'd agreed to ring on the telephone. In reality, both Barry and I didn't see Paul as a legitimate option, mainly because of the budget he needed. And on personal terms he'd recently been offered over twice what we would pay him, and in all honesty we were hoping for him to let us down. When we rang him he'd obviously had a phone call from Adam Pearson, the new chairman at Derby

County. They were just about to let Billy Davies go and were considering bringing Paul in. He had also spoken to Birmingham City and the Republic of Ireland, so he was obviously in the market. We guessed that he was likely to go to Derby and left it at that. So in our search for a manager we were now down to just two - Steve Davis and Owen Coyle.

Barry met with Steve Davis in the afternoon. We both knew Steve well so I left it to Barry to go through the details of the job with him, before we went on to interview Owen again in the evening. We had agreed to meet with Owen at Barry's house in Ribchester at eight. He'd been playing in a legends tournament at the weekend (Owen not Barry) and then driven up to Scotland for training with St Johnstone before driving back down to meet us. I had noted that he wasn't scared of putting a shift in.

I met Owen at the petrol station by the Tickled Trout pub in Preston and then drove him on to Barry's home. When we arrived Barry was as convivial as ever and we just sat in his lounge drinking coffee and chatting about the club. We talked about our expectations for Burnley and whether it would be the right move for Owen. I have to say he looked very serious, certainly compared to how he came across before, and how assured he is in front of the television cameras now. But he was just as clear in what he was saying. Owen is immediately likeable, but what came over in that hour was his immense desire to get the job. We all went through our thoughts again and within an hour he was back on the road up to Scotland. As he left we told him that we'd ring later on when we'd made a decision.

Barry got us a drink and we sat down to chew things over. We both liked Owen, but Barry had his chairman's hat firmly on and initially wanted to play the safer card and go for Steve Davis. That would be a popular appointment with the fans and local press. I can't think of any player we've had over the last twenty years who has earned the same level of unqualified respect from our supporters. There's no doubting Steve's leadership quality and my view was that he would indeed be a Burnley manager one day. But I thought that he needed to serve his time working closely with a really good manager and gain his confidence that way. I thought that it might just be too much too soon for Steve, so I was trying to push Barry towards Owen. I argued that we needed some 'non- Burnley' thinking, and from a football and financial point of view, the opportunity to source players from Scotland and Northern Ireland seemed attractive to us both. We both liked Owen and we felt that we could work with him. So, half an hour later, we decided that was it.

When we rang Owen to tell him that he'd got the job he was still in his car heading towards Carlisle. We were on a speaker phone so that we could both give the message and I started:

"Owen, we're just giving you a ring because we've come to a decision.... we'd like you to take the job Owen."

Thankfully, we hadn't misjudged his desire and he didn't say he'd come back to us:

"Fantastic ..... I won't let you down."

And something made me feel that he wouldn't. I'd seen and heard enough in the few hours that I'd spoken to Owen to make me think that we might just have struck gold. The things that differentiated him from the others were his insatiable hunger and his personal standards. Owen already had that steely determination that you don't often come across. I always believe that the guys who have come close to achieving a lot as players, but who haven't won many major trophies, turn out to be the hungriest of managers.

Owen plainly showed a desire for success that all winners have. Sir Alex Ferguson has an unbelievable hunger and he constantly needs to satisfy an inner drive. But for players who have had a glittering career and won lots of medals, it's difficult to keep that impetus when they move into management. The best managers in England over the past two decades have had an irrepressible desire to achieve heights that they didn't as players, and that has driven them to the top of the game - Ferguson, Mourhinho and Wenger. And now we had Owen Coyle.

♦

The following day we had a press conference booked for two o' clock. Barry spoke to Steve Davis in the morning and I rang Peter Reid. It was quite early when I rang him, about eight I think, but I wanted to get him early. After our interview the day before Peter must have somehow left feeling confident that he'd impressed us. So much so that he'd put it about the market the he was on his way to Burnley and the press had taken the rumour! It was all over the Lancashire Evening Telegraph, 'Reid is the Favourite'.

When Peter picked up the phone it sounded like I'd woken him up:

"Peter, it's Brendan Flood at Burnley."

"Oh .... hiya son."

"Obviously we'd like to thank you for coming to the interview and we've got a lot of respect for you," I continued. *"We're sure you'll have a successful spell back in football wherever you go, but we've decided to go for another candidate."* Silence. *"So apologies if we've had to disappoint you Peter."*

"It's not that Owen Coyle is it?" he asked.

"Well I can't really say," I replied, *"Anyway, I'll see you around Peter."*

"Okay cheers son," he cheerily proffered, and then he hung up. I immediately thought to myself, 'Imagine being in charge of him and being called 'son' all the time!' That would have been a strange one.

I must admit that after we had made our decision I was quietly panicking. And when we rolled up for the press conference there was a sense of, 'well we're all glad that you've made a decision, but who's Owen Coyle?' and I have to say my heart didn't exactly leap when I heard someone asking if St Johnstone was a full time professional club.

But the more I focussed on the decision, the more I became convinced that Owen was head and shoulders above the rest. As the press conference got going my conviction grew and became stronger even than it had been the day before. So much so, that I went as far as to call him a 'young Bill Shankly'. That was one of those moments when you hope that you haven't said something that will come back and bite you in the backside. And I remembered what Dave Whelan had told me. This decision could send the club the right way or the wrong way. But we already felt that we could trust Owen, and if things didn't always go right it wouldn't be for the want of trying. We just needed to give him the right resources in terms of finance and support.

◆

There was a good buzz about the place again when we turned up for Owen's first game in charge, at home to Stoke. They were riding high near the top of the league and were serious contenders for promotion. The fans really got behind the team again and the players deserved it. We drew 0-0 but we played a lot of free flowing football, something that we hadn't seen for months, if not years. It looked like the players were relaxed. It was very encouraging but although we deserved to win the match, we hadn't, and after the game I resolved to follow the next few matches closely to see whether I needed to plan a trip abroad!

As the weeks went by, when I watched Owen in action I noticed a big difference. Steve Cotterill worked very hard on knowing the opposition, but he frequently became concerned about them, how they played and how good they were compared to us. And often, that fear of the opposition seemed to dictate the way we played. Owen's philosophy is to let the opposition fear us, let's just go and play and do the best that we can. That helped our players to relax and to concentrate fully on what we were doing.

Which was a good thing really, because our next two games were away to Watford, who were top, on Tuesday night and then away to second placed Charlton on the Saturday! At Watford the players carried on where they left off playing some good attacking football. We didn't look like we would settle for a draw when we were holding them at 1-1, and then a good start for Owen turned into a dream start when Joey Gudjonsson hit a cracking winner.

That week was as exciting as anything I'd experienced as a Burnley fan because it meant so much to me. It was as good as the two previous ones had been awful, and I felt a welcome fusion of relief and delight. And it had a perfect ending when we went to Charlton and won 3-1. Bloody brilliant - what a start!

As I stood holding a glass of wine in the director's lounge at The Valley twenty minutes after the final whistle my phone went off. It was a text from Phil Gartside at Bolton which simply read:

"Bleeding Hell!"

8

Bump

December 2007 – May 2008

'The art of leadership is saying no, not saying yes. It's very easy to say yes. Tony Blair

From the moment he set foot inside Turf Moor Owen Coyle looked the part. He had steely determination, clear direction and an unbelievable level of personal fitness. The players very quickly understood what he expected from them, and he engaged a striking willingness from them to follow his remarkable work ethic. He cannot understand the mentality of players who are happy to pick up their wages even if they don't make the team, probably because he'd spent his own playing career sweating blood for the cause and wishing to play football. He just believes that is wrong. But on the whole he had inherited a good squad of players and some great leaders, like Steve Caldwell and Graham Alexander, who bought into Owen's way of thinking from the outset.

He has an infectious enthusiasm and a smart sense of humour, but the crucial ability to keep himself and his players grounded. In short, we were going to have success at some stage but it would be bloody hard work and the objective was to be the best that we possibly could be. Owen's way of working on the training ground matched everything that we'd been trying to do off the pitch and I knew that this was a huge piece of the jigsaw firmly in place.

And Owen's teams play without fear. By all accounts he had created a fantastic spirit up at St Johnstone and his win ratio of 50 per cent was up there with the best managers of all time. Every manager has an opportunity when they arrive at a new club as players are keen to impress but I don't think anyone envisaged our struggling side playing the division's top two teams and beating them both.

Owen quickly gained a foothold and effortlessly struck up a warm rapport with the fans who could see that our style of play was changing and that the manager talked a lot of sense. His early interviews on Radio Lancashire were upbeat but not unrealistic. He knew where we needed to improve, but from the very start he was at pains to tell of his absolute faith in the ability of our players. We knew that in time we would have to get some better players in, but each member of the current squad had the manager's belief and support.

But as every long suffering football fan knows, when things are looking good, there's inevitably going to be something, or someone, looming on the horizon and preparing to dampen our spirits. And as every Burnley fan knows, when we've recently destroyed the best teams in our division, the last fixture we want is a home match against the bottom club!

So a couple of weeks before Christmas we had a Tuesday night home fixture against QPR and as tradition dictates this was the match that was sure to kickstart our poor run. To be fair it's usually Boxing Day when our early season promise begins to disappear. I'd like to hear from any Burnley fan who has eaten a turkey curry and a selection box on the same day as we've picked up three points.

Anyway, we duly managed to lose to QPR 2-1, which had the effect of lifting them off the bottom of the table to be replaced by Preston North End of all teams, who we happened to be playing at home the following Saturday. This was another chance for us to lose to a lowly team. If it wasn't so tragic it might be funny.

So our players lined up against Preston, desperate to right the wrongs of the previous Tuesday, and blissfully unaware of what was to follow. But the referee gave us a hint in the first minute when he denied us a clear penalty right in front of two thousand astonished Preston fans. You wonder if you're suffering a form of neurosis when you are convinced that we always get a bizarre refereeing performance when we play North End. The Turf Moor choir adopted the chant 'We only get shit refs' as a protest. But anyhow, we had come out all guns blazing and I thought that surely it would just be a matter of time before we got on top.

So it is hardly surprising that after 96 topsy turvy minutes we left the field with nine men and an excruciatingly poor 3-2 defeat.

That was bad news, and around the club and town expectations had already started to fall as people began to accept that this was the beginning of our seasonal bad run. For Owen's part, he was getting used to the Championship and the level of competition. For us, a top half team, to lose at home to the bottom two teams was a realisation that all the teams in the Championship are capable of beating each other.

♦

After Christmas the transfer window opened and with it came the usual rounds of speculation and fears. Supporters naturally want the best for the club and when we are in a mid table position they want us to kick on, so many shout that now is a time to invest in new players and not to sell our best assets.

Part of the philosophy that we had committed to as a club was that we would try to get some younger players for the medium term, and where possible get the best value that we could for older players. And so if you do get an attractive transfer fee offered for an older player it can be commercially difficult to refuse. At that time one of our most valuable players was Andy Gray, and at 30 years old he fell into that category. But he was widely known to be our best hope of scoring the goals. So when he confronted Owen with a transfer request it set off a trail of negative publicity in the local press. Our fans sometimes get frustrated when we talk about selling players and the older ones hark back to the seventies when we had a conveyor belt of talent coming through the youth team and we became known as a selling club. But despite all our undoubted pride in what we achieve at Burnley there are commercial realities that we wrestle with and sometimes we need to make tough decisions to try to safeguard the club's future

It wasn't particularly well handled from Andy's point of view because he had spoken to Owen before we had actually received an offer, so we knew that he had been approached secretly and that, in financial terms, a very attractive proposal had been put to him.

When Owen rang me he was concerned that Andy was going to go, but we hadn't received an offer for him so to all intents and purposes we were in a state of limbo. But Owen didn't want to play him in the home game against Plymouth that Saturday because he felt that Andy was simply in the wrong frame of mind.

And sure enough, the following day I had a phone call from Charlton who wanted to offer us a million pounds for Andy. I had already agreed with Owen that, as Andy had emotionally committed himself to going to Charlton, we'd have to achieve a price of around two million to satisfy ourselves, and also to give us the money to find a replacement.

The bidding with Charlton started and we received an offer of one and a half million that would go up to two million with add-ons. While we were chewing that over I received a call from Andy's dad, Frank Gray. I had been in a conference that afternoon and when I picked up my messages I saw that I had three missed calls from Frank. When I rang him he was literally pleading with me to let Andy go because he knew that this was going to be his last significant move. And in all honesty any one of us in Andy's shoes would probably have wanted the same thing, so I couldn't blame him for trying. But I knew it would make a dent in the confidence of the fans as well as making Owen's job harder.

When I talked it over with Owen and Barry we decided that on balance we would have to let him go, because if he stayed he would probably be distracted from his commitment to the club. He had enjoyed an outstanding period at Burnley and always worked hard, but once a player's head's been turned it can affect the team if you don't deal with it one way or another.

So we agreed the deal with Charlton and Owen quickly got to work on finding a replacement and it soon came from a familiar source. We've always had a good relationship with Sunderland. It's a similar place to Burnley in some respects, with its working class mining heritage. Our backroom team know their management staff pretty well and so if a player's available there we often get early notice. And when it was hinted that Andy Cole might be available on loan Owen was immediately interested. He's got a good eye for strikers and with my 'fan' head on Cole appealed to me as well, in the same sort of vein as Ian Wright, an evergreen centre forward who could quickly prove to be an effective recruit.

We couldn't afford his wages though; but Andy wanted to come to Burnley, he hadn't played many matches at Sunderland and they were happy to loan him to us, so we agreed to make a contribution of half of his salary. Owen wasn't worried about Andy's match fitness because he knew of his recognized professionalism and when he scored on his debut in our win against Scunthorpe the signs were good. I thought, in a similar way that Wrighty had, Andy might galvanise us or at least bang in ten goals.

A couple of weeks later we went down to QPR and I think our forward line of Akinbyi and Cole must have worried them! We managed to stick four in including a Cole hat trick in a 4-2 win which gave us new hope that we might be capable of reaching the play-offs.

By the middle of March we were still in touch with the leading pack and about four points off a play-off spot but it had all been a bit stop-start. There were still rumblings around the town following Andy Gray's departure and when Charlton visited Turf Moor for a Tuesday night match I suspect he knew the type of reception that would likely greet him. Burnley fans are fiercely loyal to those who they feel have returned their loyalty. Steve Davis always had a standing ovation when he visited Turf Moor with Luton, Luke Chadwick wasn't quite so lucky. On this occasion the reception wasn't hostile, but neither was it friendly. We won 1-0 and the first time Andy got a cheer was when he was substituted. There was a certain irony that Andy had gone off to the so-called big spending London club who we then beat at Turf Moor, and it wasn't lost on our fans. It's funny how things work out sometimes.

From our point of view, it had ratified our overall strategy to go for younger players and take profit on players who didn't necessarily have a long term future with us. We had justified our decision and did so even more when Charlton were relegated the following season. The same could be said of the sale of Wayne Thomas, the circumstances and outcomes were very similar.

When we beat Charlton we'd given ourselves the chance of a promising finish and we were looking forward to the visit of Wolves the following Saturday. I met Steve Morgan, the Wolves owner and chairman, in the boardroom. Steve's a friend of mine and when I asked him how he felt about the game he said:

"Not great to be honest Brendan. We're giving it away every week. You could beat us today."

'Excellent,' I thought. It was unusual for Steve to be downbeat and he's not one for daft mind games. And we'd been playing pretty well on the whole and Gabor Kiraly was in form which was giving our defence more confidence. He'd had a good game at Stoke the previous week and then had a clean sheet against Charlton. But in the meantime he must have lost the strength in his pants because in the opening minutes of the match against Wolves he proceeded to let a weak shot through his legs. If that wasn't enough, a few minutes later, under no pressure whatsoever he smacked a clearance against Michael Gray who gleefully slotted it past our hapless keeper. Defensively it was a bad day at the office, and somewhat miraculously we kept the score down to a 3-1 defeat.

Owen was apoplectic with rage. It was the first time that I'd seen him really annoyed. He was disgusted with the defensive performance and vowed never to play Gabor Kiraly again.

And he didn't. It was bad news for Gabor, but it gave Brian Jensen the chance to re-establish himself, so I suspect there's a sizeable number of Clarets fans that with hindsight can look fondly back at that comic display, although it didn't seem so funny at the time.

And nobody felt any better when we lost 2-1 at Preston the following week, so I decided to cheer myself up by flying down to Carrow Road to watch us play Norwich. To be honest, I really wanted to experience Delia's cooking at the match. On the day there were about eight of us travelling down there, family and friends, but only two could go into the boardroom to enjoy the Delia experience, so the other six went into another hospitality lounge.

I settled down in the boardroom with my brother Steve, anticipating whatever mouth watering delight was on the way. But when it actually arrived it wasn't all that good. It was like nouvelle cuisine from the eighties, a tiny breast of chicken with baby carrots and a potato. It was hardly befitting of a football match. So I was disappointed with the Delia experience and more so when we met the other lads who'd been in the hospitality lounge and had a real feast!

Every time my brother Steve had been to a match over the past couple of years we had lost 2-0. So to pass the time at lunch I had a twenty quid bet with him that we'd lose by that scoreline. Of course we did lose 2-0 and I did take the money off him because we agreed that would probably get rid of the curse....

♦

Owen had a lot on his plate. He'd been at the club almost six months and while there was clear progress in the style of football we were playing, we just weren't consistent. And one player was worrying Owen more than the others. Wade Elliott had improved beyond recognition over the last couple of years. When he arrived as a tricky winger from Bournemouth, he clearly had ability but didn't always beat his man. His confidence had grown and the quality of his distribution was great and he had won the 'Player of the Year' the season before. He was probably the best player this year as well. But the problem was that Wade's contract was up at the end of the 2007/2008 season.

When Owen arrived in November he quickly got his head around the quality of our squad and concluded that Wade was a vital player, and one that he definitely needed to retain. So over the course of January, February and March Owen was continually trying to persuade Wade to re-sign but without success. Wade's a lovely lad, very intelligent and conscientious and he's popular around the club. And he's a modest guy. I remember when he went up to collect his 'Goal of the Season' award at the Midland Hotel in Manchester the presenter asked him to describe his goal, which incidentally was a screamer against Charlton. Wade pondered for a second and then said:

"Well... Blakey knocked it inside to me and I hit it with my wrong foot and it ended up in the net. It was a bit lucky really."

Every week the players have the opportunity to review their Prozone efficiency statistics with John who manages the stats, and Wade is one player who always takes the opportunity to check his output. He's keen to get the very best from his ability and fitness levels. Another regular in John's office is, predictably, Graham Alexander, who is presumably preparing himself to play until he's 45!

But I think Wade was a bit reluctant to extend his contract having not been offered an extension the previous summer. He's certainly not the type of lad to put cash before football, but he had some justification in wondering whether he was appreciated at the club as much as he should have been.

Owen and I were getting more and more concerned about the situation because, come June, he could walk away for free. On the one hand that was bad business for the club, but equally importantly, on the pitch he was probably the most creative player we had. All in all, to lose Wade would be a desperate blow to the team.

As we were getting more worried about Wade, I coincidentally met his agent, Gary Mellor, at the Stoke City away game in March. Gary and I instantly hit it off. This was the first time I'd spent a lot of time with him, and subsequently we've become good pals. That has probably been beneficial to both me and Gary and to the football club over the past year or so.

When I met Gary, I was trying to understand what we needed to do to keep Wade happy and Gary told me about his sensitivity at not being offered an extension the previous summer. So after the Stoke game I spoke to Owen and offered to talk to Wade as a fan/director.

Owen was willing to give it a try so I went to see Wade at the club in Owen's office. We sat down and speaking as a fan I told him what I thought he needed to hear:

"Wade, putting aside the money, I've got to tell you how the fans feel about you. We love you. You are going to be a Burnley legend, because we appreciate wingers and you're an eye-catching player."

Wade was listening carefully and I think inwardly hoping that I wasn't about to ask him for his autograph, so I carried on:

"I know as a footballer the grass is always greener, but you'll never get this type of relationship with the fans anywhere else."

Wade was still taking it in but he didn't really comment. He smiled so I went on:

"I think as a club we made a mistake when Steve didn't offer you a contract in the summer. But Owen believes in you totally and while he's our manager I know that you'll always be one of the first names on the team sheet."

I told Wade that one of the reasons I was sat in front of him was our ambition to be a Premiership club:

"We're not just happy to survive in the Championship. That's the view from the top. We're going places and we see you as a fundamental part of that plan."

In order to right the wrong, I told Wade that whatever financial number we agreed we'd backdate it to the start of the season. Wade received that well. I think he felt that he'd got an apology from the club for overlooking him when he had one year left on his contract and he had won 'Player of the Year'.

And when he signed his new contract that was a big moment for us in bringing together a team that we thought could challenge. You need committed players who are popular within the team and who can win a game, and Wade is all of these.

Up until then I had never been to see any of the players regarding their contract terms, but Owen felt like he'd tried everything he could think of and it was a last throw of the dice. I can't underestimate Gary Mellor's role in this. A good football agent always has to act in the player's interests but should take time to understand the character and strategy of their players' clubs to explain clearly what it means to them. Gary had listened to our plans, interpreted them as sensible and given Wade a positive recommendation to stay. May 25th of the following year confirmed the significance of Wade's commitment to the club and we knew he had a big part to play in Burnley's future.

◆

Back on the field, in some ways we were lurching towards the end of the season, and by the time we played our last home game against Cardiff City we were well out of the play-off hunt. Fortunately it was an exciting game for the neutral, we sacrificed a two goal lead in a 3-3 draw and the Cardiff defender Darren Purse took a chunk out of Andy Cole's leg, before Cole chased the red – carded Purse up the tunnel to demand an apology! The Welsh FA (surprisingly) later rescinded Purse's red card to allow him to play in the FA Cup final. But for all the family entertainment, when I looked at the game seriously I couldn't help thinking that we were too easy to break down, and we certainly had work to do to prepare for the following season.

But before that we had our final game of this season away to Crystal Palace who had already qualified for the play-offs. So it was a good opportunity for us to go out on a high note against a team that was already looking ahead to more important games. But it didn't turn out as we hoped and expected. I don't know exactly what went wrong, we had a few players in the team who were out of contract but so does everyone else at the end of the season. We were a bit shaky in defence to say the least; Michael Duff was coming back from injury and he struggled, and Clark Carlisle was sent off after about five minutes. We basically capitulated and finished the season with a 5-0 defeat against a team that was preoccupied by the aim to avoid injuries at all costs. It was a disappointing end to a promising season.

When I spoke to Owen on the way back he said that it had been so bad he felt physically sick. And I believed him. I could tell that he was hurting. So we agreed that we'd meet first thing on Monday to discuss how we could change things around for next season. We both knew that we had to get going immediately if we were going to have any chance of being really competitive in three months time.

9

Dream Team

May - August 2008

'If God had an agent the world wouldn't be built yet, it'd only be about Thursday.' Jerry Reynolds

The first full season of my involvement at the club had been anything but uneventful. We'd started with high hopes that we could do well. Steve Cotterill had brought in several key players and we were beginning to put together a team of leaders. When the season began we were much stronger than twelve months previously and I was cautiously expecting a top ten finish or better.

The main event of real significance was when we changed the manager. And after arriving in a blaze of anonymity Owen had made a good start all in all; we finished higher than the season before and that had to be progress. In my capacity as operations director, off the pitch I had encouraged the senior management team to generate an atmosphere of togetherness. Our communication links were improving and I felt that we had a more professional feel about the whole place. Over the past nine years or so Barry had done a brave job in first saving the club from oblivion and then transforming us into a proud Championship outfit. But he had held it together and in 2006 he had needed someone else to invest new money and energy to progress the club. And in that first full year retail sales had improved by over 30 per cent at a time when attendances weren't increasing, so I knew that we had the people in the club to make positive progress.

And we had signalled our ambition by announcing our plans to undertake a £20m redevelopment of the ground which would bring the stadium up to Premiership standards and improve our commercial and retail offering. I had also been to see Paul Fletcher the chief executive of Coventry City. Paul had built up his reputation as a stadium expert and I knew that it would be great to have him back at Turf Moor. He's just the sort of additional positive influence we needed, and a very popular figure in football circles. So early in 2008 when I saw on Sky Sports News that he had resigned I sent him a text saying:

"Paul – don't forget if you fancy a cup of coffee and coming down to Burnley, give me a shout."

He texted me the next day and so a couple of weeks later I went to see him at his home in Rawtenstall. We talked about the club's plans to redevelop the ground and the things we had been trying to do off the pitch. We got on famously and I was really pleased when he agreed to join us in a redevelopment role, and also to take on some of the chief executive responsibilities. I had to be hands-on in the first year, partly because of the money that I had invested, but I also recognised that it was important to create a commercial team for the long haul.

We also invited Anthony Fairclough back as commercial manager. He had gone to Wrexham as chief executive, but I hoped to bring him back to the club, as everyone spoke highly of him. He's a proven quality relationship manager and a real team player, so he would fit the model perfectly. Wrexham had a bad season and were relegated out of the Football League, but even so Anthony had increased revenues substantially. Wrexham's bad luck was good luck for us and I called him to ask whether he was interested in a return and he immediately snatched the opportunity.

By early summer, the credit crunch was biting hard and there was a general reticence on the board to provide financial support which put our redevelopment plans on hold, so that was the perfect time for Paul to formally take on the role of chief executive. I was pleased that Paul was back and felt that his presence was a massive boost to us at senior level. My agenda was all about getting positive forces in the club and Paul was experienced in football, charismatic and well connected. The more positive people we had in the club, the better the feel good factor and the better the club is perceived by the outside world. So in the end we had attracted arguably the best CEO in football in a roundabout kind of way, and with Anthony in his team I had real confidence that the business could now support our determination to improve results on the pitch.

The last burning issue that Paul, Barry and I were desperate to address was finding someone to head up our Centre of Excellence and bring that forward as part of the bigger picture strategy. I was happy that we had stronger characters in the first team now, but knew that our future policy must be to bring young players into the club and to grow our own talent, as we had done repeatedly in the sixties and seventies.

We talked to a few people about the role including Brian Flynn. He's another Clarets legend and has fantastic knowledge of the game, and was doing a great job of managing the Wales under-21 team. But when Paul went back to Brian a couple of weeks later he wasn't so keen. He got the impression that Brian felt a bit jilted because we hadn't offered him the job immediately, when at the time we were only considering the appointment as a new investment and needed time to make a decision.

Barry suggested we talk to Martin Dobson, another former team-mate of Fletch's. Barry had been at school with Dobo and knew that he still lived in Bolton. At the time he was scouting for Ipswich, but he had previously been in charge of Bolton's academy. So Paul lined up a lunch for me to meet Martin and I was looking forward to it. When it came along I was like a kid in a sweetshop. It was me, Paul Fletcher and Dobo, two of my childhood heroes sat at the table. I was thinking, 'I can't believe this. Here I am with Fletch and Dobo and they're waiting for me to say what I want to do!'

Martin is a real gentleman with a statesmanlike presence. He has very high standards, can be fairly uncompromising if he needs to be, and has a real passion for the club. Burnley had given him the chance when Bolton had rejected him and after we sold him to Everton he went on to play for England. As we talked I started to notice that his favourite expression kept coming up, which was 'big dos and little dos'. So big dos and little dos we took him on!

Martin had the ambassadorial status that we needed and the existing youth development team, Geoff, Terry and Vince immediately benefitted from the experience and structure that he brought. In order to be competitive at youth level you need people who are strategic and can look after the best young players day and night and also maintain a close dialogue with their parents.

So by the summer of 2008 the operational team off the field was Barry and me at board level, Paul Fletcher in as chief executive, Anthony Fairclough on commercial sales and Doug Metcalfe and Chris Gibson running their teams. Darren Bentley on the media and PR side is a distinctive presence and the club wouldn't be reflected in the same light without him. Ken Stout as finance director was a safe pair of hands and now that we'd brought in Dobo on the youth development side I felt that we had a really good group of 'can do' positive people with the capacity to become a Premier League Club off the pitch.

♦

Owen and I had been discussing how to improve the playing squad from the Monday after our last game of the season. Locked in the chairman's lounge we had pondered over the various player issues and started by looking at the squad that had collapsed 5-0 at Palace to decide who we wanted to retain. It had been Owen's first season and I think he felt inclined to keep John Harley and James O' Connor because they'd both given their all for the club and he was reluctant to make the tough decision of letting them go. Having had the benefit of watching them from the stands for the last three years I felt that they weren't top six players and we needed to get better. Owen agreed and decided to offer them both a shorter new contract and if they didn't take it up they could go. They both found clubs quickly. John went to Watford and James to Sheffield Wednesday. We talked about Alan Mahon but Owen didn't see Alan as a regular as his form had been indifferent.

The goalkeeping position was a worry for us. Brian Jensen's contract was up and we had a long discussion about him. He'd had a mixed season but we both felt he was the right type of player for the club. He occasionally had an off day so we needed to bring in some competition and Owen was determined not to play Gabor Kiraly!

Owen had brought with him a list of players that he wanted to pursue and at the top was Martin Paterson, the promising striker who had scored 15 goals for Scunthorpe as they were relegated from the Championship. Then he had Kaspars Gorkss the Blackpool centre half, Chris Eagles at Man United, Andrew Driver at Hearts and a keeper called Diego Penny from Peru. I'd never heard of Penny, but then I'd never heard of Owen Coyle a year ago! But Owen thought that he'd be adequate for the first team, he'd played a blinder for Peru against Brazil and Owen had seen enough evidence to suggest he had a future with us.

So we had set out on the acquisition trail and we were determined to do everything possible to get our target list of players. And on the whole we were pretty successful.

The top priority was a faster striker, and Martin Paterson was certainly that. Both Owen and I thought that he was the best young striker in the Championship. When we played Scunthorpe I had got on well with their chairman, Steve Wharton, and so I said I'd chat to him over the summer. And Martin Paterson's agent is Gary Mellor, so I alerted Gary to the fact that we might be interested in going for Martin. But Scunthorpe, being Lincolnshire country boys, know the value of a pound and they wanted two million for him. Owen had put nominal values against his targets on the list and had Martin at £500k! So we went round and round for a while, starting at £500k, then £650k, then £720k. I don't think they were getting fed up with me but Owen didn't want to go above £750k, he was naturally nervous of spending too much money, which isn't always a bad quality in a manager! Most managers are wary of spending a lot of money, if it doesn't work out you may lose your job.

But by the third week in June I received a call from a contact telling me that Ipswich were about to make a bid for Paterson and if we wanted to do a deal we should get a move on. It was a Saturday morning and I said to Ellen that I needed to spend most of the day sorting it out. From nine in the morning to seven in the evening I was on the phone to two of the Scunthorpe directors. In the end I got to one million, with £300k on appearances and a bonus if we got promoted. I was keeping Owen informed as I went on and by teatime he said:

'Well you know, Brendan I don't want to pay more than a million"

So I said:

"Just stand back and look at it for a minute. If he scores twenty goals for us next year what's he worth?"

"Three million," he replied.

"Is he going to score twenty goals do you think?"
"Yeah."

In the end Owen agreed to go with it. We had confidence in the player and to me we were more than likely paying £1.3 million for a player who'd be worth £3 million at the end of the season.

So we moved on to Chris Eagles. I agreed with Owen that I'd try to progress this because I have a business relationship with Gary Neville and Ryan Giggs. They're both super lads and for all their unbelievable success they have life in good perspective. When we're together we talk football for a good forty five minutes before we move on to business. I hoped that they would reference Burnley for me to Chris and tell him that we had big plans for promotion. Hopefully this would set the scene for Chris and give us the chance to sign him.

In due course Owen contacted Sir Alex to agree a transfer fee and then he arranged a meeting with Chris before he went on United's tour of South Africa. Owen was delighted with the meeting because Chris just wanted to talk about football, and not about the contract details. You know a player of his calibre will ultimately want to be looked after but that discussion came later. He had his priorities in the same order as Owen's.

But the deal hadn't been cemented and on the South Africa tour Chris was top scorer for United. Then one evening I received a text from Gary Neville saying, 'I'm sat next to Chris Eagles at dinner and I've put in another good word for you!' Which was all we could ask for I guess.

Owen had got his agent to make sure that Chris could come up to the club the day after he returned from South Africa and after a bit more assurance from Owen he signed. Sunderland had been interested in Chris but I think it helped us that Roy Keane had said some things in the press that Manchester United hadn't liked!

It was a huge coup for us to get these two players, both young with bags of potential and both desperate to play football. We'd secured them for less than three million and were sure we'd got great value.

The one player we missed out on was Kaspars Gorkss. Owen met his agent, who is his father, a couple of times but he went to QPR, probably with different priorities to Paterson and Eagles.

We did sign Diego Penny as goalkeeping back-up. He had been introduced to Owen by a trusted agent. And then a huge young talent called Kevin McDonald came in from Owen's Scottish contacts. He's been heralded as a great prospect for the future and so Owen was very persuasive when he went to see his parents. We paid Dundee five hundred thousand and we had another young powerful player in the squad.

Then Owen turned his attention to defence and particularly in creating competition for left back position following the departure of John Harley. He rated Christian Kalvenes at Dundee United as the best left back in Scotland and once again set about using his ambition for the club and determination to get his man.

♦

The plan had been to assemble faster, stronger players in all areas of the team. And the biggest signing, in many ways, was our hard earned success in getting Wade Elliott to stay, he's such a prolific creator of goals and he's like grease lightning over ten yards. And he wanted to play in a side that could win trophies, so when Owen and I sat down with him in March I assured him that we were looking to improve the squad as quickly as possible.

Now that we had assembled a better team the next thing to do was to enable the manager to keep the same squad together throughout the year and not to sell anyone. At board level that's quite daunting when you know that you're going to lose between four and five million in the financial year. By August I thought the board would be apprehensive, which wasn't surprising when you compared our financial activity that summer to previous years. But I'd researched all the clubs that had gone up over the past seven years and I knew that to have a fighting chance you had to have enough strength in depth and that meant a higher wage level, and now we were heading towards eight million. We thought we had a few players that we could sell or loan out but didn't know when that might be.

Reducing the wage bill had frustrated Owen as he had to spend a lot of time and effort trying to move players on and that can hamper incoming activity. Our wages were higher than they'd ever been at the club by a mile but in order to get on you need competition between better players. We had made a strategic decision to go for that, but that brings with it the risk that you might be stretching yourselves to get to where you want to be.

As a stop loss I proposed a formula that we would seek to cover our losses by three times in the value of our squad. So if we lost five million we would need the value of our squad to be fifteen million, so we could sell one or two players to cover the loss. When we valued the squad at the start of the following season we came up with a figure of sixteen million and that was after we had plugged the loss from the previous year with an excellent sale.

Kyle Lafferty had come up through our centre of excellence and made something of an impression over the past couple of years. And because he was tall and performed consistently well on television, he had earned himself a reputation that was slightly better than the average Burnley fan's view. He was sought after nationally but on a game by game basis he wasn't consistently one of our best players. Kyle's potential was debated regularly within the club and the consensus varied, but my view was that he wasn't a natural goal scorer. He just didn't appear to have a cool head for finishing. I debated this with Owen but he was fearful of underselling Lafferty and wanted to get four million for him. But he knew that we needed to recycle some money to get better players and we were still looking at last year's loss. If we got three million for Lafferty we'd be able to cover last year's loss.

So we started to discuss our plans with the parties who had already expressed an interest, Fulham, Wolves, Celtic, Rangers and Ipswich. On the final Friday when we were trying to settle the bids the key bidders were Rangers and Celtic, which was great fun for Owen, playing the 'Celtic Rangers' game!

Celtic wouldn't go beyond about two point nine million and Rangers made it up to three and a quarter. Owen still thought that was light but both Barry and I thought that was a good measure of the market which dictates the value of the player. We'd talked to all five parties from the outset and this was his market value. So all in all, it was a great result.

♦

As part of the strategy for moving the club forward we knew that building relationships overseas had to be a priority. And also we hoped that our pre-season tour would reflect a positive image of the club and excite our squad. I learnt from Gary Mellor that Adrian Heath was the manager at Austin Aztex in the American Soccer League, so I rang Adrian to see what he thought about the talent pool out there. He thinks that within five years it will be better than in the UK, so we decided to tour the US in the close season and in May 2008 Barry, Paul, Sandy Stewart (Owen's assistant manager) and I went over to make further contacts and finalise the itinerary. We were prepared to move quickly because if we waited for every other club to build relationships over there we'll be last in the queue for talent. I wanted us to get the pick of the crop early on, and if you're going to achieve that status then you have to make the effort to go and form relationships.

We went to see Minnesota, Carolinas and Richmond who all had teams in the USL, the equivalent of the Championship in the States. We needed to get an idea of how we could source players from over there, as the game has increased in popularity and has become the third most popular sport in the USA. There's already been a pattern of top quality goal-keepers coming from North America and with their love of hand ball sports that will surely continue. But also they seem to have a surplus of big, strong players defensively. So with the objectives of sourcing new talent and organising an exciting pre-season tour we headed off to the States.

The highlight of the tour was down in Carolinas where they looked after us very well and we felt that we could form a relationship there. That later evolved into us working with the PDL team (the 18-21 university team) which has now been branded the Cary Clarets. We stayed in Carolinas for a few days and got to understand a bit more about the league structure and players' backgrounds and nationalities before we moved on to Richmond.

We'd adopted Paul Fletcher as our driver. Paul thought that Barry and I had deliberately not taken our driving licences when he ended up doing all the driving. But he got his own back on me at least, because the long road trips between the clubs were filled by an endless stream of quiz questions. Paul and Barry both love quizzes! All Sandy and I could do was to try to punctuate the tedium with sporadic jokes.

After the success of our visit to Carolinas we discovered that there are some disparities in US football which became apparent on our visit to Richmond. After a long journey we arrived in Richmond on a blistering hot day to be met by the chief executive of the club, a big guy called Frank. We met in downtown Richmond where Frank had agreed to pick us up. As we all looked around wondering which his car was, he wandered towards a very battered old truck. This struck us as being unusual as everyone we had met so far had luxury cars and were keen to make an impression. Barry smiled at me and whispered:

"This doesn't look promising."

The Richmond's club offices were at the head office of Krups, a grocery business in the States. Krups had adopted the football club as a community project. When we entered the huge office building Frank led us up to the meeting room to give us a presentation with his coach and administration assistant. Even though the head office was immense we ended up having the presentation in the photocopying room where the sandwiches were sat on top of the photocopier! It was a bit of a tight squeeze for the group of seven present and a sorry lack of air conditioning added to our discomfort.

As the sweat patch on Frank's shirt visibly grew, we glanced among ourselves, using the telepathy that Barry and I had developed, and Paul and Sandy had grasped, and decided to make this as quick as possible. We had allocated an afternoon for the visit but the tempo of our questioning indicated that we would be out of the door within an hour.

To be fair they had done a very enthusiastic presentation to us and so we felt that we should in all courtesy ask a few questions. So I said:

"Who is the most successful player you've ever produced at Richmond?"

Frank thought for a few seconds and replied:

"Lindsay Roberts."

"Is that a woman?"

"Yeah."

In the States women's soccer is very popular and I don't think that Frank had quite figured out why we were there. We made a sharp exit!

♦

We arranged our pre season tour to the USA and set up fixtures against Carolinas Railhawks and Minnesota Thunder. And for the players it was fabulous. They had got used to going to Austria and the Isle of Man, and so to go to the US was thrilling. The training facilities were excellent and the hotels were three or four star. And the football clubs hosting us made a real fuss of our players. They had pre-match ceremonies with national anthems played and firework displays. It was great fun and there was a real buzz about the squad. Everyone enjoyed the experience and the players thought it was the most successful tour we'd ever had and represented great preparation for the coming season.

I couldn't go on tour because I had other commitments but I wanted to see the matches and our game with Carolinas Railhawks was videoed live on the USL website. It came out at about two o'clock in the morning over here and I decided to stay up with my son Kevin to watch the match. Armed with our biggest pot of coffee we went online to tune into the game, but it turned out to be the most frustrating match I'd ever watched. Not in the sense that we were as crap as we were when we kept tripping up over the ball against Rochdale some twenty years ago. The problem here was that as we downloaded the match, every minute or so it froze on the internet. We waited three or four minutes to download it again and then a minute later it froze again, so I gave up at half time. We lost that game 2-1, which on the face of it wasn't a spectacular start for us, but more importantly it showed that there was a competitive pool of talent out there. We had played most of our first eleven and so I was pleased we had made the effort to research the USL.

I didn't bother trying to watch our game with Minnesota and was ready to pick up with Owen when the team returned. We were both happy that the whole process from Crystal Palace through to the eve of the new season had been productive. We had implemented a detailed plan to strengthen our squad, to have a notable pre-season tour and be ready with a confident bunch of players. We had analysed every player decision by asking ourselves the question, 'Is he a top six player?' And having signed experienced guys with leadership qualities the year before, our agenda had become more about youth, pace and power.

The players had come together really well and were already showing the type of team commitment that we had been looking for and they were ready for our first fixture, away to Sheffield Wednesday.

10

The Red Devils Never Miss

August – November 2008

*'Ever tried. Ever failed. No matter. Try again. Fail
again. Fail better.' Samuel Beckett*

The credit crunch started in earnest in July 2007 and
over the past twelve months it had become clear that not
only had the UK banks lost confidence in each other,
they had also run out of money. From the moment that I
detected a change in the wind in early 2007 I had
implemented a strategy at Modus to de-risk. Later that
year we were in advanced discussions with RBS Private
Equity, to whom we had offered 20 per cent of Modus
Ventures, my development company, for £30 million.

When RBS ultimately withdrew from the deal in
January 2008 it became clear to me that the domestic
banking sector was seeing some stress and so I decided
to go beyond the UK. During the Summer I had a knock
on the door from Macquarie, the Australian shopping
centre and food store business with interests all over the
world. Their team in London approached us as they were
interested in buying into Modus, on a similar basis to the
deal we had agreed with RBS. They were keen to come
to an agreement and submitted their proposal to their
investment analysts. But the response they received said
as much about their company as mine. They could see

the synergy and Modus was a good fit for their business, but they had some 'challenges on their own capital'.

UK institutions were out and Australia was struggling so I went to see my South African partners in our shopping centre division. I explained to them that the market was changing at a furious pace and that we needed to de-gear, so they introduced me to their preferred investment partners who happened to be Lehman Private Equity. That seemed to be a good introduction as Lehman had done a lot of big transactions and held an elevated position in the US financial sector. So we met with their team, they looked at our projects and we did a roadshow of our shopping centres. A few weeks later they came back with a response from their investment committee, and the shiver I had felt twelve months ago became a full on freeze. They said that there might be internal difficulties at Lehman. And six weeks later we saw the iconic images of investment bankers in London carrying their files out of the collapsed bank's UK head office.

During this trail of disaster we had been trying to fund a large new build shopping centre in Newport, South Wales. We had agreements from Marks and Spencer and Debenhams and other national names to anchor the centre. The UK banks were unable to contribute to the project so we went out and successfully obtained board approval from Hypo Bank based in Germany, who offered us terms in a formal offer letter. A week after we'd signed and returned the offer I received a phone call saying that they were no longer able to pursue the project because they'd run out of money.

So I had chased the global downturn all around the world, from the UK to Australia and back to the US and now even Germany had come unstuck. Once I had received the news from Lehman, I researched the Middle East and found that values were dropping there too. The modern global village was showing how it was all now connected and at that moment I felt the negative impact of the banking sector being on the verge of collapse.

I realised by the beginning of the new football season that my development business was about to be hit by a tsunami.

Project commitments were based on exit values that were beginning to see a 40 per cent drop, and once the distressed banks started to analyse that for themselves they changed their policies very quickly. So when I saw Lehman go bust I knew a brutal financial crisis was on the way.

♦

Within the scheme of things the world economic crisis was cataclysmic but during the close season, while the team was off on tour in July, something happened that hit me harder than anything else could. I hadn't gone on the tour because my mum was dying of cancer. When Mum passed away Dad, who is my Burnley 'watching partner', was at an all time low and as a family we were devastated.

♦

Against the backdrop of economic meltdown and its direct affect on Modus and with deep personal sadness the oncoming football season once again provided a welcome diversion. Having had a great pre-season, where the team had already developed a vibrant togetherness and will to win, the expectations were higher than usual. We'd added some excellent young players to a squad that already had strong characters and plenty of leadership and there was a perceptible confidence in the camp.

Doing my own analysis of the team I thought we were definitely good enough for the play-offs. I travelled to our first game away at Sheffield Wednesday with

Kevin and we both felt excited and optimistic. It was a beautiful sunny day and hordes of hopeful Burnley fans had turned up. The first day of the season isn't going to turn all your ambitions on the head, but you always want to start well to give the fans an early boost. But within three minutes of déjà vu for all Burnley fans we were 2-0 down! After all our pre-season harmony that was a disaster, and then the game followed an inevitable path. We briefly looked like we might pull it back before they got the third and from thereon we were simply hanging on to our reputation.

The following week we were at home to Ipswich and there was huge excitement, as there always is for the first home match, and it was a chance for us to eradicate the memory of the week before. I wanted to propagate the excitement so I hired the Red Devils to do a display before the game and then land on the pitch. From our research we had learned that anything coming in from above is apparently spectacular to fans because you're looking up, which you don't often do at football grounds. Admittedly I'd done it the week before but not out of excitement!

I wanted to put on a show for the fans and it was a magnificent sight as the first four red devils appeared as tiny dots in the heavens, before zooming into view and landing expertly on the pitch. Then as we were watching the fifth parachutist come down Clive Holt, who's our health and safety director and was stood next to me said:

"I think he's going to land on the roof."

Not wishing it to be the case I said:

"Are you sure?"

Clive was watching with an increasingly alarmed look and then he confirmed:

"Oh my God – he's going to land on the roof."

As the parachute deflated, the parachutist lay prostrate on top of the Cricket Field Stand. I don't think the Red Devils have ever missed before and I just couldn't believe my eyes. Then, to make matters worse, asbestos sheets started to drop down from the roof into the away stand. Fortunately Ipswich had only brought a taxi full so that was good. Thank God there was no one below!

The home fans didn't let us down. They cheered as each of the first four Red Devils landed and then there was an ironic cheer as the fifth one crashed.

I had some important guests from Norwich Union with me and I think they were all as bemused by it as we were. We immediately had to kick into health and safety mode, but what do you do in a case like this? The one thing you don't expect the Red Devils to do is to mess up the display and it wasn't even windy!

Chris Duckworth, always ready to make light of a disaster, quipped:

"One thing's for sure, we aren't going to get a parachute payment now are we?"

So while my heart was sinking, Chris carried on throwing jokes at me and all I could think was, 'Why on earth did I bother?' Fortunately Clive swung into action to ensure that what was a farcical predicament didn't turn into a black comedy. We had to get a fire engine to drive across the adjacent cricket ground and eventually we got him down, but the kick off had been delayed by forty five minutes. Throughout the whole charade, which was being covered with impressive verve by Sky Sports, I was receiving endless sarcastic texts from pals saying things like, 'Sky News reports parachutist drops into Turf Moor after distributing leaflets throughout from the sky saying 'Kilby and Flood Out'!' So a lot of people clearly enjoyed the entertainment but it wasn't quite what I had planned.

In fact the fate of the fifth Red Devil effectively crushed any ambition I had of extending the pre match entertainment for families. Among our less successful events, we had hired Chico to sing on the pitch. He was very quickly chased off by chants of:

"WHO ARE YA? WHO ARE YA?"

And then he fell back on his 'housewives' favourite' tag by shouting back:

"Ask your missus!"

Even better was the blimp we hired to float above the pitch which was secured by a fine rope tied to the leisure centre. The local handy lads decided to cut the rope before the match and the blimp disappeared into outer space, much to the delight of the national press and our fans on Clarets Mad. Rumour has it the blimp landed on Venus!

The Ipswich game itself was never going to be as spectacular, but worse than that it simply followed the pattern of our match at Sheffield Wednesday the week before. We conceded a fairly early goal and you could see the confidence draining away from the team and we ended up losing 3-0. We never really looked in any shape at all. And on the day we only attracted 11,000 fans for the first home match of the season. After all the marketing effort we'd made and all the players we'd bought that low gate put the mood of the town into context. We were used to Championship football, and the mood of 'It'll never happen 'cos it's Burnley' has hung around the football club for a long time. The only statement we could make to change that perception would have to be a footballing one.

The Sunday morning after that game was one of the lowest times I'd had since becoming involved at Burnley. It was only two games but I had been so hopeful with the amount of effort we'd put into the pre-season in trying to get the right team. All the hard work we'd put in behind the scenes to have a memorable first home game had literally crashed. In those first two games we were devoid of confidence and any expectations we had were now somewhat deflated. Owen said that it felt like the worst two weeks of his life, he was really feeling the pain of failure at a very early stage.

We took our medicine and when the dust had settled a couple of days later we remained convinced that we still had a good squad. In the matches to come Owen changed the tactics slightly and we started to play the 4-5-1 system to make sure we could get more possession in the middle. And things started to pick up slowly but surely. We won our first point in a 0-0 draw at Palace which we could have won but for a strangely disallowed Chris McCann goal in the second half. And then we beat Oldham 3-0 in the second round of the League Cup. I stuck my neck out in my next programme notes for the home match with Plymouth, saying, 'I'm absolutely certain that this season we will attain our highest position for many years' before we drew 0-0 and Chris Eagles was sent off.

The first real sign that we were on the right track was the way we played at home to Blackpool at the beginning of September. The passion we showed and the quality of football we played against a big physical side made the statement that we could beat tough, hard working teams with our pure ability and mental strength. In previous years that type of game would have ended up in a draw. We had started to see some of the new players making a difference, Paterson especially.

The following week we had our third round League Cup match at home to Fulham. Owen approached this match in the same way that he does all others. He wants to win the match whether we're playing in the league or the cup, whether against Bury or Arsenal. And this gave us a chance to gauge our progress against a premiership team that had spent quite a lot of money. On the night we played some good football and started to display the qualities that would emerge as the season unravelled. We kept hold of the ball well, and we showed that we had a lot of pace up front with Eagles and Paterson, and Wade Elliott. They are all incisive players. But the night will be remembered for the arrival of Jay Rodriguez when he came on a sub late in the game. He's a Burnley lad and our fans always want to see local lads in the team, but to have a local boy with the talent that Jay exhibited when he scored our winner with a cool finish after rounding the keeper was almost too much to hope for. And that moment gave Jay the platform to grow. Off the field he's a nice lad, he's still a teenager really. But on the training ground he had a good relationship with Ade, after Ade had taken him under his wing. Ade's influence with a lot of the younger players has been valuable, and something he doesn't really take enough credit for.

But Ade didn't look like he was having the best season himself and we needed somebody younger to work with Martin Paterson up front. Owen had looked around at different options and on the Sunday before the last day of the transfer window he rang me up and suggested Steve Thompson at Cardiff. I knew that we were over our wages budget at seven and a half million pounds and we'd be heading towards eight, but we did need a bigger presence. So we decided to try to get him on loan but when Owen talked to Cardiff on the following Monday they wouldn't agree to a loan. They were happy for us to speak to Steve, in the hope of coming to an agreement with the player before the close of business. Owen and I agreed that I would be unavailable to take calls on the Monday afternoon. So as Cardiff were ringing up to see if they could get a fee out of me, they were asking for £300,000, Owen was doing his best to agree terms with Steve Thompson and his agent. Peter Ridsdale called me twice, but before I rang him back I called Owen to see whether he'd agreed terms with Steve, which he had. Owen was very happy with him, Steve's a 'good type' as Owen would say and he thought that he would fit in well. And he's a good strong player. Owen was convinced that he was just what we needed. We were going beyond our comfort level to get Steve in but we desperately needed a quality target man.

As luck would have it, Cardiff appeared to be so desperate to reduce their own wage bill that just by avoiding Ridsdale's phone calls through the afternoon we managed to sign Steve on a free!

♦

Clive Holt has served on the board for twenty three years and he's been with the club through thick and thin. He's a true Burnley fan and in the past has done a lot of good work for the club, overseeing with great expertise the development of the James Hargreaves and Jimmy McIlroy stands that modernised our facilities and offering to the fans. More recently he has taken on various responsibilities, including getting the erratic Red Devil off the Cricket Field Stand roof, but he was also involved in a delicate debate of principle that caused a stir throughout the club early in the season.

Clive has always supported all our players and takes a keen interest in the progress of our youth team. And for years he's watched the youth team matches at our training ground at Gawthorpe faithfully accompanied by his dog. But dogs do what dogs do, and Martin Dobson was unsettled by the increasing scattering of dog turds around the training pitches. As I have said Dobo has high standards and so, big dos and little dos he took the difficult decision to ban dogs from Gawthorpe. It wasn't anything personal and Martin is a dog lover himself.

But Clive wasn't having any of it. He'd watched the youth matches at Gawthorpe for decades with his hound, and I think to him, this was an unnecessary accession to the type of health and safety fascism that is threatening all our freedom. So he stuck to his guns, until Dobo confronted him one afternoon, pointing at his 'no dogs' sign and Clive reluctantly wandered off. But Clive is nothing if not loyal and the following week when the youth team was playing he watched from a mound across the river in the next field with his faithful dog by his side. Traditions are often hard fought and change has never been easy as Turf Moor.

♦

Back with the first team, by the time we had a well refereed match with Preston at the end of September, which of course we won 3-1, we were starting to gather a bit of momentum. And by the middle of October we were in touch with the play–off places. When we went to Coventry on a Tuesday night I thought this would be a good test of our progress as Coventry had spent a lot of money on players in the summer. I had a guest with me from Coventry City Council because Modus had a scheme there. Before the match I was on a table of Coventry fans and I jokingly said:

"Well chaps, our tactics are for seventy minutes we'll keep it tight and we'll sit behind the ball. Then we'll bring on Robbie Blake and Chris Eagles and Owen claps his hands to the players, just once, as a signal that the time has come to play like Brazil."

And sure enough, Owen brought Robbie and Chris on when we were at 1-1 and we finished the game off in great style and won 3-1! And that was the first moment that I thought, 'Hang on, we've got a real chance here.' It just seemed that from that game on, we had developed a level of acceleration, that we could play a faster game and outwit other sides. And we were having a lot of fun. A little too much in Robbie's case when, after he scored, he dropped his pants to reveal his newly branded 'Bad Beat Bob' underpants, which earned him a yellow card. Clark Carlisle had the pants made up to commemorate Robbie's dreadful form as a poker player because he often suffered many 'bad beats', which is a poker term for a bad loss, when playing cards with the lads. But Robbie wore them with pride, and following his goal that night, on every match for the rest of the season.

It was a significant night for me to reflect upon. We were still in the cup and we'd gone to a good team and won in a convincing manner and I could see that we were really gathering some momentum. Our next home match was against Reading, who were riding high and probably playing the best attacking football in the league at that time. They had retained most of the players who were surprised to be relegated from the Premiership the previous season and so far this season they were winning matches 3-0 and 4-0 week in week out. They had already beaten us 3-1 at the Madejski Stadium earlier in the month and so a lot of our fans looked forward to the rematch with some trepidation, and with good reason. On the night they played some wonderful football and in our goal Brian Jensen made several outstanding saves. The value of Beast's endeavours was tripled when Robbie hit a sublime winner in the closing minutes. What a win that was, and it was a win that made people in our league start to sit up and take notice of what we were doing. That night we had showed that we could tough it out against an excellent team, and had new Claret and Blue heroes in the making.

♦

I listened to the draw for the fourth round of the League Cup in the kitchen at home and we were all hoping for a plum draw. I was thinking, 'If we get United or Blackburn it'll be a cracker.' But one team, as a Claret, that you never think of because we haven't played them for so long is Chelsea. So when we came out of the hat with Chelsea away I thought it was absolutely brilliant. It really was like a cup final for us, and we could go down with the confidence that we were playing well and deservedly on a good run.

The whole family went down with me, including my youngest, Conor, who in all honesty has been part Burnley and part United as a fan. He's actually probably a little bit more United because we live in Manchester.

Realistically, none of us expected to go to Chelsea and get a result but we held our own in the first half, even though we went in 1-0 down after a brilliant strike by Didier Drogba. Owen threw Ade on in the second half as a Burnley fan behind us heralded him as 'the poor man's Drogba'. And then the impossible happened when Ade scored our equaliser. Just looking up at the big scoreboard on ninety minutes was good enough for me. In bright lettering it said, 'Chelsea 1 Burnley 1.' Fantastic! The lads had done us really proud and seeing us compete with one of the best teams in Europe for ninety minutes was a wonderful experience. Their team was littered with world class players, Lampard, Deco, Mikel, Malouda, the list went on. But as Owen's team always does, we played without fear; we concentrated on what we could achieve and defended with passion. And now we always know that we can score a goal.

But the players didn't think they'd done their job and when they made it through the thirty minutes of extra time without conceding a goal they'd almost scaled Everest. Chelsea had a couple of good chances to win it, but after Steve Caldwell was sent off, a section of our seven thousand fans showed that they too had taken on our new and genuine bravado singing:

"Ten men – we only need ten men!"

This situation we had found ourselves in was becoming increasingly surreal. We now had a penalty shootout against the mighty Chelsea at Stamford Bridge and the even more bizarre thing was, that knowing what a great penalty saver Beast can be, we felt that the game was going our way.

And we put our penalties away with real belief. I think our lads had all taken on the persona of Graham Alexander and, we were all on the edge of our seats, when Wade Elliott stepped up to take the winning penalty. But Wade smashed it over the bar and we all started to think it was going to go horribly wrong right at the death. But Michael Duff, who's been a fabulous presence all season, scored his penalty and history was made when Beast saved from Mikel. He'll be forever remembered for that save and this season.

I looked at Conor and I could see by the level of disbelief in his eyes that he was now truly a Claret. Every father looks forward to the day when his son is blooded as a Claret.

I'd promised my eldest son, Kevin, that if we won I'd wear my 'Bad Beat Bob' underpants, that he'd bought me for my birthday, in the Chelsea boardroom after the match. So as the legions in claret and blue exploded into a raucous celebration I looked at him and said, 'here goes' as I put them on over my trousers and we went back into the hospitality suite. We had fun with some Burnley fans as they had their photos taken with me, and then Barry came down to find me and we carried on our celebration for a while.

Barry then suggested we go into the boardroom, so up we went drinks in hand. And as we entered their chairman's lounge, humbly known as 'the Armani Suite' it was like Moses and the parting of the Red Sea. On the left hand side the Chelsea directors stood back in awe, or disgust, I'm not sure which. And on the right, the Burnley directors were enjoying the moment and joining in with the humour. As I looked round I saw Phil Gartside from Bolton and Bob Coar from Blackburn Rovers, and Phil shouted:

"You can take the lad out of Burnley but you can't take Burnley out of the lad!"

I was still laughing a few minutes later when a steward came over to me and tapped me on the shoulder and said:

"Excuse me sir, would you mind removing your underpants?"

To which I replied:

"Which ones?"

One thing they do have down at Chelsea is high standards.

I saw Alastair Campbell on the television, he was doing an interview with Sky Sports and he was saying how excited we were with the win. So I sent him a text which read:

"I saw you on Sky – you looked close to tears – you looked happier than when New Labour got elected for the first time."

He responded:

"I was!"

That shows that he too is a true Claret.

11

Capital Punishment

November 2008 – January 2009

'One fifth of the people are against everything all the time.' Robert Kennedy

It's on occasions like our memorable win at Stamford Bridge that you see in Owen Coyle how much he wants to give victories to the fans and the board. His first words to me after the game were how he was so pleased for our fans and everyone who supported the club. And he has a canny way of drawing delight out of me after big wins. Whenever we've had a brilliant performance, of which there has been a few this season, his first words are always:

"Brendan, how are we?"

And there's only ever one reply:

"Fantastic!"

Speaking as a fan of the club there was plenty to be happy about as the season progressed. At times we were playing fast, flowing football and getting some exceptional results and everybody at the club just wanted to continue in that vein. And as a board of directors we had the responsibility of doing everything we could to support Owen and the team. The week after the Chelsea win we had a meeting, and I thought that it was a good time to plan while we had the positive glow and enjoyment of our progress. I had openly shared the fact that my fortunes were becoming negatively affected by the property market and informed the board that they might not be able to rely on me for every cash call from hereon. By this point I had put in £6.5m, half of which was a formal loan agreement from my development business, which was to be repayable if the club achieved promotion or convertible into shares in 2011 if we were still in the Championship. One or two of the directors were questioning the judgement in spending so much money on Chris Eagles and Martin Paterson. The implication was that if I'd known how the property market was turning, we should have stored the money we had received on the sale of Kyle Lafferty. So when we met in November to discuss our cash requirement for January, economic conditions were bound to impinge negatively on our discussions. Cash was tight all round and I had the feeling that some of my colleagues were running for cover.

To be fair, after I had presented my Vision Document for the club the previous year I had been welcomed to the club as the new funder so I was decisive in making investments throughout the club. But the results spoke for themselves. All income streams in the club had increased significantly, we had a stronger team on and off the pitch, our youth development was back on the agenda and the new manager was having a tremendous impact. Even the reserves and the youth teams were at the top of their leagues.

We had undertaken to expand the squad, and the wage bill had gone up to about eight million pounds for the season. We had 26 full time players at one stage and I knew that we were operating at a level that we needed to be at in order to mount a serious campaign. My research of other promotion challenging teams in previous years had shown that you need a squad of at least 24 and a wage bill at a minimum of seven million to get into the top six. We had put ourselves in the zone where it was just about possible, but for Burnley that would result in a net loss approaching five million pounds a season. There was, quite rightly, genuine concern as to how we could manage that gap.

In the meeting we started to discuss how we could proceed through the season. I reiterated the formula that I had proposed in the Vision Document, that we needed to have a squad value of three times the annual loss, so that in the event that cash needs to be found you can, where necessary, make a player sale. Providing you have a good strategy for sourcing new players that's not a problem. I suggested that we may need a cash injection of one million pounds from the existing directors and I saw it as my responsibility to find the balance, either in funding solutions, introducing new investors or player trading. But we needed to look among ourselves to find one million pounds.

As I passed that discussion round the table, to a large extent it was met by some reticence. One million pounds is a big ask at the best of times but in the middle of a ferocious economic downturn anybody would baulk at the prospect of taking any sort of risk. As the discussion evolved it was quite clear that if the club needed money it would still be my responsibility.

Ray Griffiths had been very helpful to the club, and Barry had, prior to me, invested significantly over the years but generally the onus was still on me. By now I had increased my cumulative investment up to six and a half million pounds, which was the biggest in the club's history.

But as the property market fell off a cliff I was unable to go further, although Barry and I provided guarantees to the Lloyds TSB when required. At the meeting I really wanted to get to a practical discussion of who was going to invest what, but there was more comment about the size of the wage bill and the wisdom of some of our summer signings. Some directors felt that they hadn't been involved in the budgeting process for players' wages. They hadn't. We had also assumed that we would be able to get some of our players out on loan to bring the wage bill down to seven million, but that was proving to be difficult. We ended the meeting without having agreed a plan, but I had given an early warning of a discussion that would become more urgent if we failed to respond.

♦

We had a Monday night trip away at Barnsley who were struggling on the edge of a relegation battle. We were still in the top six and as our profile had risen quite sharply the Sky pundits predicted an entertaining away win. Entertaining it certainly was, but winning at Oakwell is never easy and hampered by a quite bizarre refereeing performance we failed to live up to expectations. After dominating the play we went in 1-0 down. But early in the second half they scored again, the goal scorer being one of four players who were offside, before he controlled the ball with his hand and sliced it into the net. In a rare moment of lost focus, some of our players were still scratching their heads when Barnsley went 3-0 up thanks to an amazing deflection. With half an hour to go Owen brought Martin Paterson and Kevin McDonald on and in the end we were unlucky to lose 3-2. Even though we left Barnsley with nothing again, we had showed the explosive impact that some of our young players can have. At the end of the game Owen was seething, and as we left the ground he said:

"Brendan, come with me now to the ref's room."

"Will it make any difference?" I asked.

"Probably not, but I'll feel better!"

Unfortunate refereeing decisions can have such an impact on a club's fortunes and we'd had some bad luck that night.

Next up we had Derby County at home. They had made a bad start to the season but were already showing signs that they could be threatening. Derby is a big club;

they had just come down from the Premiership and had an impressive board. The club is American owned and Adam Pearson, who helped take Hull from a lowly position through the leagues, was chairman. And what Derby County don't know about marketing isn't worth knowing. But fortunately for us marketing expertise doesn't score goals.

The soul and the passion on the football side at Derby seemed to have been lost. I felt that there were a lot of high earning players out on the pitch, but they didn't have any attachment to Derby. We very quickly built up a 3-0 lead with a smart brace from Paterson and another from McDonald, and the Derby fans were so disconsolate that they started to sing:

"LET'S PRETEND WE'VE SCORED A GOAL."

And then they all jumped up and down celebrating! That just shows you the strong mentality of the best football fans who can find pleasure in the most miserable of situations.

For my part, winning a game relatively comfortably against a club like Derby really made me feel that we had come a long way already, and we were giving ourselves a chance. And we were also still in the Carling Cup.

We had drawn Arsenal at home in the Quarter Finals and once again our match was live on Sky. A few of us had a funny feeling about the game that night because we had freezing conditions, it was snowing, and the youngsters of Arsenal might not fancy it on a cold wet night in Burnley. This is our special recipe for beating big teams - dark, wet and a scary crowd! But this time we had added another frightening weapon, our Capital Punishment media drive, designed to put the wind up the Arsenal kids and remind them that we had already dispatched Fulham and Chelsea and had a lot of fun doing it. One of the impressive things about the people who work at Burnley is that they are genuine fans, and within our media team Darren Bentley is a lively character and he always has a bag full of good ideas. And after a late night celebrating the Chelsea win Darren spawned the idea of Capital Punishment and as luck would have it we drew Arsenal.

The Arsenal Carling Cup team was receiving their own fantastic acclaim in the media by playing attractive football and they had already beaten Sheffield United 6-0 and Wigan 3-0 in this competition.

But on the night our trusted recipe worked again. Kevin McDonald looked every bit the protégé that he is by scoring the two goals, the second of which was world class. That brought a real belief to the Burnley fans, not only had we beaten Fulham, Chelsea and now Arsenal but we were having an extended run of good form in the league. You could sense that the mood among the supporters was beginning to change and everybody's confidence was rising all the way through the club. The Capital Punishment theme had really caught on and the national newspaper headlines put us up in the spotlight again. From a PR perspective the club was showing that we had a good story, with Robbie and his underpants and Capital Punishment, and we were doing well on the football pitch so we were increasingly interesting. In fact we had fully recovered from the Red Devil's calamity!

The club was a fun place to be, there was plenty of banter and the spirit in the team and club was becoming noticeably potent. There was very little to complain about really but all the time there was an undercurrent building up at board level that the change was too much. But there was growing evidence that the investment we had made in the playing squad was only just enough. On the Saturday after the win against Arsenal, we had a trip to Sheffield United, who were one of the strongest sides in the league and Owen had a few injury problems. And that was an occasion when Owen and his squad really showed their mettle. Owen played Wade, our creative forward, at full back but he wasn't fazed by having to do that. His attitude is always that the game is eleven against eleven, whoever we're playing and if we do our jobs correctly then we don't need to worry about our opponents. And that belief in his players in turn increased their belief in themselves and their team mates.

Chris Eagles had a brilliant game and took the Sheffield defence apart. Every time he received the ball you could see them back peddling and we had our first win at Bramhall Lane for over thirty years. On that day we looked every bit a promotion team. And Chris continued his great form as we beat Southampton and then last year's play-off finalists Bristol City. Owen's belief in his players was at an all time high and we went into the Christmas fixtures nicely in the play-off zone and with a cup semi-final tie against Tottenham in sight.

But we had our usual Christmas humbug, which of course is a tradition, but not one that we are really that keen to preserve. The defence started to have a bad run and it was difficult to understand why. But our seasonal dip in form this year was worse than normal, we lost five league games on a run and from a relatively comfortable position we fell out of the play-off zone. It was starting to worry Owen and it was worrying me too. All you can do as a director when things are going wrong on the pitch is be as supportive as you can, try to find ideas for the manager about how we can improve. We picked up a couple of red cards in that run and gave away a few penalties. When we went to Preston on the 17th January, we conceded two which I suppose is about par for the course for those games. Owen was pretty wound up about that. Behind the TV cameras you have to maintain an air of dignity, which Owen always does impressively, but after this game he was very upset about it and we had started to feel that we were suffering a catalogue of odd refereeing decisions. As a manager you can't afford for a victim mentality to creep into your psyche but nevertheless Owen was getting more than mildly annoyed. At one point he did start to count up the number of points that we had lost in this unfortunate way. It's becoming a bit of a tired argument, but why on earth we don't use video replays in our sport is beyond me. It works so well in Rugby League and Tennis that I don't really understand the argument against the introduction of technology to help the referees. It would certainly take one irritation away from the game.

Steve Cotterill was on the panel for Sky at the Preston match and after the game he came up to me in the boardroom and said:

"You were very unlucky today Bren, good team out there. Nine out of that team were mine you know!"

When I later told our first team coach Steve Davis he said:

"He wouldn't have said that if we were near the bottom!" True.

The following week when we lost 3-0 at Watford Owen was really fed up because our defence that night was dreadful. Unfortunately the ball was sticking in the mud repeatedly but we had gone five games without picking up a point. You can blame referees, bad pitches, and voodoo - whatever you like. But there are times when we can really only blame ourselves. After all, we were conceding sloppy goals and so in the transfer window Owen picked up a young right back, Rhys Williams, on loan from Middlesboro with the objective of strengthening that department.

In the middle of this losing run we had our cup semi-final first leg down at White Hart Lane and a chance to gather some new momentum in continuing our Capital Punishment plot. The hospitality at Tottenham was more welcoming than Chelsea, which, apart from the opportunity to wear my underpants, was quite a sterile experience. Tottenham felt more like a traditional football club. I'd never been to White Hart Lane before and when I went out into the stadium I thought it felt established and homely like Turf Moor. And the players seemed at home as well; in the first half we played some phenomenal football and throughout the half I received a number of texts from people who were watching us on television and were astounded by the quality of our football. At half time, we were leading 1-0 and after Paterson had scored we hadn't looked in any trouble at all. It looked like we were capable of going all the way.

As the players emerged for the second half the Burnley fans teased David Bentley, formerly of Blackburn Rovers, who was substituted by Harry Redknapp. They cheerfully sang:

"Where's your bastard gone, where's your bastard gone?" to the tune of 'Where's your Mama gone?'

But then, in an illustration of the problems we were experiencing in the league, our defence simply melted away. It looked like they were a bit surprised by how quickly the Spurs team came at them in the second half but they shouldn't have been. Harry Redknapp had obviously read the riot act. But you could look at each of the goals and see individual errors and so it was hugely disappointing to go home with a 4-1 deficit in a two leg semi-final.

Owen's sentiment before the return leg at Turf Moor was that we should go and enjoy the game. We all felt we might win but could we win by the three goals that we needed? Even though we were three down there was still excitement in the town as this was the first major cup semi-final we had experienced since the Newcastle game in 1974. I had booked a hospitality room in the Jimmy McIlroy Stand behind the goal and I was looking forward to a good night. I hoped we'd do ourselves proud and I genuinely thought we could win on the night but didn't think we would pull the deficit back. Everyone in football had written us off but once again Mother Nature had provided the ideal circumstances – it was a dark, cold, wet and windy night and our crowd was at its hostile best for the arrival of our southern opponents. Just before the kick off, a freezing downpour swept across the ground and the Spurs players shivered. We had a full house and the scene was set. A special level of vitriol was, yet again, reserved for David Bentley and so his every touch was booed. The atmosphere was unbelievable from the outset but when Robbie scored with a trademark spectacular free-kick the noise and the passion in the crowd went up ten notches. Fans all around the ground were pinching themselves and each other when Chris McCann made it 2-0 with over ten minutes to go. Our players were at their best, Robbie was tormenting the Spurs defence as we launched wave after wave of attack and with about five minutes to go we had the most magnificent and most electric moment that we had all experienced for many a season. Young Jay Rodriguez hit his striker's goal with such a style that it seemed he was the only one in the ground with a cool head. The whole place went absolutely crazy; people were falling over each other celebrating, hugging and shouting. This was the most incredible and emotional comeback many of us had ever seen. The feeling of elation that I had then will stay with me for a very long time.

Unfortunately it was too much for one elderly fan who suffered a heart attack and died happy after the third goal.

We had got to extra time and with our away goal we just needed to avoid conceding and we were through. As time ticked on we didn't seem to be in any trouble, and we were pushing on for another goal. We didn't look like we were going to concede a goal and I started to visualise Wembley against Manchester United and I wondered what that might feel like. With about three minutes left Ellen said to me:

"Wow, if we get to Wembley against Manchester United .... I wonder what sort of outfit I should wear!"

As soon as she finished her sentence Tottenham scored. And I felt the same agony that everyone else in the ground felt, apart from the relieved and surprised Spurs fans. But the most remarkable thing was that as soon as Tottenham had scored all of the Burnley fans got to their feet all around the ground and gave the team a standing ovation and, as Wembley dreams escaped us, we kept the Burnley spirit by singing:

"Oh Burnley we love you."

That showed the passion in the town that is behind the club and is difficult to emulate anywhere else in the country. Owen said to me after the game that it was the best atmosphere he had ever experienced in his career:

"The hair was stood up on the back of my neck Brendan."

It was a memorable night and in some ways it was enjoyable, but the underlying feeling was that it had left us with a painful sense of disappointment which we had to put right.

◆

With the Carling Cup now behind us, although still on everybody's minds, we wanted to draw strength from the pain and the manner of our defeat and the town's pride in the team's heroic endeavour. We were desperate for a win in the league and had a worryingly familiar opportunity when bottom placed Charlton came to Turf Moor. It looked for the entire world that we were going to do our usual trick when we were 1-0 down with quarter of an hour to go. We had been playing well and looked capable of winning so when we equalised the lads threw the kitchen sink at it and finally in the 96th minute we had a 2-1 win. That sparked a celebration so loud that it was evident that everyone in the crowd knew just how vital it was. We were on the way again with a crucial three points.

When I thought about it, the wins against Charlton and against Southampton in December struck a chord with me. These were two big clubs that had been in the Premier League in very recent history and they were now both struggling in a relegation battle. It illustrated to me that in football money is not a guarantee of success. Southampton had been big spenders the previous season, including buying Wayne Thomas off us for one million pounds. I recalled that when last we visited Southampton the board seemed to be somewhat detached from supporters of the club. The club's decision to bring Sir Clive Woodward in when Harry Redknapp was their manager seemed a little odd not only to the Southampton fans but to the rest of the football world.

When Charlton came to Turf Moor I felt that there were some similarities between the two clubs in that there was nobody on the board who demonstrated a real touch for the football side and you have to have that in a football club. You need the final decision maker to really understand the sport and I believe that was one of the main reasons why both of those clubs were in danger of dropping down into the third tier. I was curious to know how such big clubs seemed to perform well operationally in terms of marketing and hospitality but they hadn't done well on the football side. I think I had my answer. It takes months to make £100,000 operationally but it only takes a minute to lose it on average player wages. Exceptional players are worth every penny but being able to identify them is the key at Board level.

And we had our own challenges up at Turf Moor. At the turn of the year there were a number of things flowing through our minds in the boardroom with our objective being to keep the team together to try to get promotion. But to achieve that we needed to raise cash from other sources. Throughout January at every match I attended I was pressed by one or other of the directors saying, 'we won't sell anyone will we?' It was a sentiment I shared but we did need to find some capital to fund our requirements between February and May. Even after the cup runs we were probably going to have reduced budget losses approaching three million pounds. The options were a player sale, director's capital, discounting TV money for the following season, securitisation of season tickets or bringing in a new investor. And there was a new fund that two investment managers from Goldman Sachs were running with the Emirates Bank that would soon be available, branded the Hero fund, which allows clubs to raise money against the value of their players.

I had already introduced a procedure whereby the club always has an up to date Investor Prospectus available, so that if anyone suitable was interested in investing in the club, they would have access to the club's statistics and the latest due diligence. Substantial investors usually show their interest and then very quickly move on if you're not ready for them. We initially produced this prospectus because we'd had some tentative interest from an offshore investor. Ultimately if you harbour ambitions of being in the Premiership for a sustained period you have to have some deep pocketed shareholders these days. At Burnley, we would rather have somebody who was within a group of owners so we were open to suitable parties who would be a partner at board level rather than a new owner of the club.

Paul Fletcher had a contact in the US who had previously shown some interest in Coventry City through a corporate finance guy called Shaun Peak (for the sake of privacy the names have been changed for the book). Paul met with Shaun and an interested party called Mark Goldman of Byman Partners. Mark was a New Yorker and a typically hard nosed businessman. And a discussion evolved where Mark expressed an interest in investing in Burnley. At about that time we were considering whether or not to sell a player. We thought that this discussion might come to something and so Mark flew over to England to meet us on the eve of our home match with Swansea City early in January. We put him up at the Lowry Hotel in Manchester and arranged to drive him round Burnley the following day and then take him to the match. I picked Mark up at Piccadilly railway station and took him to the hotel where Owen was due to come and meet us for a drink. Then after that, Mark, Barry and I planned to have dinner while Owen went home and got some rest in readiness for the Swansea game.

When I introduced Mark to Owen, as they shook hands he quickly said in his New York pronunciation:

"Owen, you remind me of somebody."

Owen smiled and said to him:

"George Clooney?"

"No, no not George Clooney."

"Yeah yeah, George Clooney." Owen was insistent. Then he thought for a second and added:

"As a matter of fact I was in a film."

"You were in a film?" asked Mark and I couldn't wait, if slightly anxiously, to see where this was ending up.

"Oh yeah, it was a film called 'A Shot at Glory'."

"You were in 'A Shot at Glory'?" clearly astounded.

"Aye. Me and Sandy were both in it," replied the redoubtable Scot.

"You know 'A Shot at Glory' is one of my favourite films. I've watched it five times!" Mark was delighted.

Barry and I were spectators for the next thirty minutes as Mark quizzed his new found hero.

We had dinner and then Mark decided he wanted to stay in Burnley to get a feel for the area. So we put him up at the Oaks Hotel on Colne Road and then we arranged to pick him up the following morning to take him to see our training facilities at Gawthorpe before going back to Turf Moor. We hoped Mark would get a favourable impression of the area because we all knew that long term financial support would be good and we discussed a figure of fifteen million pounds, which would really help a promotion challenge this season or next. The interest was still at a very early stage and in order to avoid too much discussion in the boardroom I suggested it might be better if Mark didn't say who he was and to pretend that he was a friend of mine visiting the country. Mark was agreeable to this:

"Sure, no problem Brendan, no problem at all."

That afternoon as I walked into the Chairman's Lounge it was already quite busy, the Burnley directors and families were to the left and the Swansea City group to the right. As I walked in I announced myself:

"Good afternoon everyone, how are we all doing?" and then I pointed to Mark as he came in to introduce him, at which point he stood in the doorway and said:

"Hi there, my name is Mark Goldman. I entered a lottery competition in New York for the opportunity to watch a Burnley game, and I was the only entry so here I am!"

It wasn't quite what I'd planned. And as we sat at the table to eat our dinner, everybody was quietly surrounding us to try to listen in to the conversation, so we kept pausing as we spoke. It was all a bit bizarre and then the game resulted in a 2-1 win to Swansea in front of a fairly modest crowd and it was a televised game. Barry and I were trying to put a brave face on it but in a way it was a disappointment for all of us. We thought that our investment discussions might all come to nothing because of the result on the day, and I think Owen was disappointed as well because he was hoping to get a win for us to prompt some further investment.

After the game I gave Mark a lift back into Manchester. He was flying out the next morning and on the way back he said:

"Brendan, at the end of the game I was looking at Barry, and I'm afraid he looked like a sorry puppy dog. I suppose Barry might think this would affect our decision to invest."

I replied:

"Yeah, we probably both feel like that."

"Well no Brendan. We're still very keen to further the due diligence and talk about investing for a fifty per cent stake in your club."

So we were left with a positive view and the discussions moved on. In terms of the other cash options for the club we'd taken the brave decision not to sell anybody, which in retrospect was possibly braver than we should have been. With Championship overheads Burnley really does need to trade one or two players per season to survive. We were hopeful for the Mark Goldman investment coming to fruition at some stage, but we also looked into the possibility of releasing some capital through the Hero Fund. But all of this involved change in the normal club operations and that was the biggest difficulty that I had faced on the board. If I hadn't been there I expect we would have sold some players and kept the wage bill below three and a half million because that was the safest strategy. What I was trying to do was to make the club an attractive proposition all round to enable us to bring in quality players and significant long term investment. Football is a global business and there are several ways of bridging cash to finance well run clubs.

But luck was on our side as well. While exiting the Carling Cup we had made our way to the fourth round of the FA Cup and had achieved a creditable 2-2 draw away at West Brom. We always fancied ourselves for the return. West Brom are a footballing side but they were struggling to finish teams off in the Premier League and if anything they were the underdogs for the replay at Turf Moor. We won 3-1 and it was a more significant result than people realised because that earned us an away tie at Arsenal in the fifth round and the revenue to us was the best part of one million pounds, at a time when we really did need it. So while every possibility was being explored to bring in new investor capital, we saw that sometimes football is a game of luck, and we were certainly lucky to draw Arsenal when we did. That windfall bought us the time to look at other financial options. Barry and I focussed our energy and initiative to find the solutions.

In our January board meeting we had calculated the amount of cash we needed until the end of the season, which after the cup draw was roughly speaking about another million pounds, assuming no deal was made with Mark Goldman in the meantime. There are ten directors on the board so I suggested we keep it simple and all find one hundred thousand each to keep everything ticking over. It wasn't a comfortable meeting and I didn't get the response that I'd hoped for. In the end Barry, Ray Griffiths and Mike Garlick put together seven hundred thousand and Barry and I gave personal guarantees to the bank to back a six hundred and fifty thousand pound overdraft facility. Latterly John Sullivan had also offered to assist with a loan of two hundred thousand pounds but ultimately it wasn't required.

At the end of the season we were to revert to the options of drawing cash from the Hero Fund or furthering our plans with Mark Goldman. His investors had decided to invest if we stayed in the Championship. And with a quality playing squad we would inevitably receive offers for players in June, after all the high profile matches we had enjoyed.

Up to that point, and since my first board meeting two and a half years earlier, I had been able to step forward to principally underwrite the position for the club but because of the problems I'd suffered with my development business we needed to share the responsibility as a board. It was really difficult. Barry and I needed the cooperation of everyone on the board because of the decision that we had all taken not to sell a player. At this point, the funding commitments by the four of us kept the club going at a vital stage in its history.

About this time Barry and I discussed the possibility that the board needed more focus to make key decisions efficiently, and that a ten man committee was impractical. After me and Barry, Ray Griffiths had provided the greatest financial support to the club. So the three of us arranged a lunch to discuss how we should go forwards.

Ray had started life as a market trader and then became wealthy by founding Target Express, the national distribution business. He was 78 and had many years of business experience behind him. We were both Rossendale men by upbringing, and being from that neck of the woods he was a straight talker.

We hadn't always agreed on certain subjects. When we re-signed Ade Akinbiyi Ray was very annoyed. And later he told me that the big screen in the Cricket Field Stand was, 'A bloody waste of money!' We had got the screen to demonstrate to sponsors our ability to offer a full range of media options and it also improved the match day experience for most fans. But Ray was adamant that the difficulty in getting money out of folk in Burnley would make it unviable. In some ways I knew he was right but I wanted to drive the club's aspirations and ultimately to improve the feelgood factor all round.

When we met to discuss the Board and future funding, Ray was in good form and agreed that the executive decision making committee needed to comprise a small number of directors. He didn't mince his words and he summed everybody up in two sentences and when he branded one Director as "an after darker, no bugger knows what he does", Barry and I were in stitches. He concluded the meeting by agreeing to contribute to the cash call and I will always remember him for his generosity and sharp tongue, which made him a uniquely memorable character.

Ray sadly died on 16th July this year, but his contribution to the Club's promotion was essential.

12

Congratulations Dobo. You've won an Embroidered Club Scarf!

February – May 2009

'If you can keep your head while all around you are losing theirs ... then you'll be a man my son.' Rudyard Kipling

It was a big relief for all of us to return to winning ways against Charlton and West Brom, and we had another severe test awaiting us with an away match at Birmingham followed by a home game against Wolves. Playing the top two could push us one way or the other. There were signs that we were on the right track again but we needed to strengthen our resolve. And in the first half at Birmingham we showed that we had that inner strength and we completely dominated the game. We were one goal up for most of the half and it should have been more. Then, just before half time, Steve Caldwell and Brian Jensen had a moment of madness and contrived to let Kevin Phillips in to get an equaliser. We had to settle for a draw but overall we had shown how, when we are on form, how much better than the teams around us we were. And we were good enough to beat the league leaders Wolves the following week which gave us the confidence to attack the next few games. It looked like we'd recovered from our winter wobble and we were back in the hunt for a play-off place.

While Owen and his team were working hard to continue their improvement on the pitch, around the club Paul Fletcher was using his charisma, purpose and acumen to ensure that all our commercial activities were maximising value. And Paul always has time for a laugh, and in one outstanding moment of inspiration he came up with a wheeze that sent shock waves through the club. Paul made a list of his '100 Greatest Clarets" in no particular order, but gave it credibility by positioning Jimmy McIlroy, Jimmy Adamson and Leighton James at 1,2 and 3. He then had himself at number 10 and all of his seventies team-mates between 50 and 100.

All of the 100 ex- Clarets then received a letter, enclosing the list, on Burnley Football Club headed paper which read:

Dear Mr...

As you may have seen on the local TV and Media, the Football Association Heritage Committee has asked for a random set of our supporters to vote for their all- time top 100 players and this has been organised under the title "100 Greatest Clarets".

Over 5,000 season ticket holders from Burnley FC were picked at random and asked to vote for their top 100 players of all time, from the many players who have represented the club over the last 49 years since 1960.

The results are now collated and ready to forward to the FA Heritage Committee for a supplementary pull-out to the annual FA Heritage Yearbook which celebrates its 50 year anniversary in 2010.

Awards for the winners will be presented at a special 'Top 100 Clarets Awards Ceremony' (in conjunction with Preston FC, Blackburn Rovers FC and Rochdale FC) at the Grosvenor House Hotel in London on

01.04.2009 commencing at 7-30 prompt. The evening will be covered by 2BRadio, Granada North West and Sky Sports News.

The Awards
- **The Top 10** *players at each club will receive **an engraved gold omega watch (value £2,586.00)***
- *The Top 11 -20 players will receive **an initialled Harrods leather briefcase (value £296.00)***
- *The Top 21-35 players will receive **an inscribed port decanter (value £75.00)***
- *The Top 36-50 players will receive **two Burnley F.C season tickets for the season 2009/2010***
- *Those players voted 51-100 will get a limited edition club scarf.*

On behalf of the Heritage Committee I do hope that you will be able to attend the awards night and congratulations on being nominated one of Burnley's Top 100 players.

Yours Sincerely

Out went the letter with the top 100 list. The players who didn't spot the date of the awards ceremony went variously ballistic. Personal pride in an ex-footballer can be a very funny thing. Colin Waldron who scored the goal to take us to the 1st Division in 1973, and was 90th on the list couldn't believe that his fellow, if more modest centre back, John Pender was at 66. Martin Dobson, who was at 64, just below Ron Futcher and Kurt Nogan, was apparently less than impressed. I'm told he said to Vince Overson:

"If they think I'm trailing down to London and back for a scarf they've another thing coming!"

And over at Old Trafford, Sir Alex was trying to persuade Mick Phelan his number 2, who was Paul's number 95, that he should really go to the ceremony and not snub the fans. When the Claret's Mad website got hold of the letter the message board went bananas. The main focus of fury was the fact that Robbie Blake wasn't even on the list and one angry thread had over 100 contributors decrying the inclusion of Ted McMinn and Gazza at number 6 when Robbie wasn't even in the 100.

Paul's not yet recovered from the fallout of that but I doubt it'll discourage him much in future.

♦

When you look at Sheffield Wednesday, you have to say that compared with Southampton and Charlton they are doing a good job. The club is still saddled with almost thirty million pounds of debt and the manager, Brian Laws, is doing well with limited resources. The wage bill is much lower than the league average at round about five million. But for them to follow Wolves to Turf Moor and hammer us 4-2 after they'd beaten us 4-1 at Hillsborough earlier in the season didn't feel quite right. I thought that when we had lost at Watford the defence was too porous and we saw the same evidence again. For us to maintain a challenge for a play-off place, that was something we had to sort out. Owen was particularly keen to beat Wednesday as he'd felt punished on the opening day of the season. This was a game he really wanted to win to avenge the early defeat. And it was at a crucial time of the season.

Our goals against record was poor relative to the other teams in the top half of the league table and we still didn't seem to be picking up the pace we really needed to have a play-off finish. We had an opportunity to get on the right footing the following Tuesday at Blackpool. It was our first match in March and it was a filthy night, and not a very comfortable one for our supporters who had braved horrendous conditions to cheer us on. Blackpool's ground is like a throwback to a time when all football clubs had an open end or two for the hardiest fans but it's quite unusual these days. It was blowing a gale and at one stage it took Brian Jensen five minutes to take a goal kick. Every time he reset the ball it blew away. There was then a lengthy discussion between the referee, Owen and Tony Parkes, the Blackpool manager, about whether the game should carry on. Owen wanted to keep the game going because we didn't want a backlog of fixtures and he felt that the lads were up for it on the night. Clark Carlisle had returned to the team, having been rested for a period and in the desperate conditions his presence was immense, he won everything on the night and I hoped that he'd keep that form to take us through the season. Christian Kalvenes had also started to settle into the team more and he scored a late winner that sent our windswept fans home happy. It was a really significant win for us and notably a clean sheet. The back five we had of Kalvenes, Carlisle, Caldwell and Williams, with Graham Alexander sitting just in front had stopped us from conceding a sloppy goal. If they could carry on in that vein we had every chance of success.

By this stage in the season we had attracted a lot of interest in the national media, not only for our cup exploits, but also for the style of football we were playing. And people had noticed that we had already played almost fifty competitive matches. Only Manchester United in the whole league could match that and it brought us great recognition. Naturally, pundits were commenting that with a small squad they feared that we would eventually run out of steam, but our group of players were forging such a strong bond that they didn't notice. They just wanted to play more football. The experience we had against Spurs gave the players, the club, the supporters and the town a real thirst for success.

The trip to the Emirates for the fifth round of the FA Cup gave us another taste of life at a higher level. As ever, Owen wanted to go and win the game. There was no thought of resting anybody so that we could concentrate on reaching the play-offs. Owen decided to put his strongest available team out because he felt that this was a match we could win. He was confident of getting a result but equally he had picked up that Arsene Wenger had been annoyed with the defeat he had suffered at Turf Moor and wasn't going to play a weakened team.

The stadium at Arsenal is fabulous and it's a memorable experience to go there as a fan. But I felt in the boardroom area that it was rather like an up market canteen. There were about a hundred and fifty people in the boardroom, all sat at tables, with no interaction or moving about the room. It seemed to me that it was being run to make money but very little of the personality of the club had been retained. I have picked up from our travels to Premier League grounds this year that some clubs like Spurs have retained their character, while others have sold their souls to the commercial world. West Brom is a good club to visit when they have the pre-match dinner, the chairman and chief executive of each club sit together and they can have an informative two way discussion. At board level it's important to advertise the club's ambition and share knowledge and it gives you a better idea how the club operates from top to bottom. There's less of that in the Premier League but I think it's still important.

At the Emirates Wenger's determination was soon evident by the quality of his starting line up and Eduardo scored a beautiful goal in a game where I thought we acquitted ourselves admirably, but on the day we simply couldn't match their quality.

♦

In consoling ourselves with the old adage, 'we can concentrate on the league now' we had one clear objective remaining. And the way the players responded to our defeat at Arsenal was nothing short of remarkable. We had two home games to follow. The first was on the Tuesday night against Crystal Palace with Neil Warnock flying their flag. The match was a typical Burnley thriller and to get a 4-2 win after being 2-0 down in the second half was a massive step towards the play offs. We always play better in the dark! Steve Thompson scored a brilliant goal to make it 3-2 and everyone seemed to have their tails up. When I spoke to Owen I could sense that there was a huge confidence and belief from his side that we were capable of much more. The team spirit was excellent.We had the right mix of players and with the cup competitions out of the way you could see that there was a single minded determination within the club.

The team's confidence was now unshakable and the following Saturday they put on a carnival display of football against Notts Forest. Forest were managed by Billy Davies and he never gives anybody an easy ride but we were unstoppable. We scored five spectacular goals, including a Robbie free kick, a Joey Gudjonsson rocket and a wonderful curling strike from Jay Rodriguez. We had set a bit of a marker down and nationally people had noticed that we had stuck four in against Palace and then five against Forest. In fact, we had scored nine goals unanswered in less than one hundred minutes.

The following week we were away at our old friends Plymouth and with spirits still at a high we went 1-0 up, before a couple of our younger players became victims of their own confidence. Rhys Williams and Chris Eagles were playing one touch keep-ball in our penalty area and when they lost the ball Plymouth gratefully scored. Owen was beside himself at half time but we secured a 2-1 win with a Robbie 'special' from twenty five yards.

As we moved into April we could see the finishing line. We were still in a play off spot and with a four point cushion between us and seventh place. We calculated that we needed ten points from our last six games to reach the play-offs. Owen was still driving the team on to aim for a top two place. Wolves were almost there but Birmingham and Reading were both inconsistent and the second place was up for grabs for any of the next four that could win their remaining games. In our run-in we were able to measure ourselves against Cardiff and Sheffield United, who were both in the top six and both harboured strong ambitions to achieve automatic promotion.

We picked up a draw at Derby and a home win against QPR, but then on Easter Monday we conceded two late goals at Cardiff to lose 3-1. Owen was mindful of the marathon season that he was asking his players to complete and decided to ease the burden for our most senior player. At 37, Graham Alexander is an outstanding example to younger players of what can be achieved with a combination of ability, discipline and determination. Owen had substituted Graham at Derby when we were 1-0 up and again against Cardiff at 1-1. It's a measure of the man that our defence relies so heavily on him but Owen was right to expect that we can perform equally well when we have to change things around. We need to be adaptable and flexible. But clearly we couldn't underestimate the influence of Grezza

As the season had gone on Owen had got himself into an extremely focussed mindset about how we were going to play, and in his interviews you could see that he was in battle mode. He was both determined and confident that we had it within ourselves but the Cardiff game perversely was a time when I just wondered if we'd thrown it all away. And admittedly I was afflicted by a slight touch of envy. It occurred to me, while we sat in the old Ninian Park, that the following season Cardiff could be show boating it in their brand spanking new stadium in the Premier League. The Welsh Development Agency is very supportive of Welsh projects and it turned out that the club had got the stadium virtually for free. And in the boardroom, they have a fairly complicated mix of shareholders and lenders including

Sam Hamman. Our boardroom is a kindergarten compared to theirs. When the game was over there was a lot of back slapping among the Cardiff directors and a clear expectation that they were going to end up in the top two. Nobody quite expected their wheels to come off as spectacularly as they did.

To make matters worse for us, our old rivals Preston had surprised more than a few by going on an impressive winning run, and amazed absolutely everyone in football when they beat Cardiff 6-0 on the following Saturday. This put them only one point behind us before our Monday night fixture with Sheffield United, the first of our final three matches. I hoped that the defeat at Cardiff was enough of a shock to our system to give us that extra focus for our final three games.

I've known Kevin McCabe, the chairman of Sheffield United, for many years. He's a very successful man in the property sector and on a personal note, there's no one I'd rather lose to. But on that night I so desperately wanted to win that I told Kevin I didn't want to see him before the game. We only spoke at half time and full time. It was televised and being a night match it was all blood and guts. Paterson scored a great goal for us and then Clark Carlisle and the rest of our defence stood magnificently against the bombardment from the Sheffield team. The 1-0 win was just the tonic we needed to finish well.

So we went into our final two games with a four point cushion and when we travelled to our last away fixture at Southampton it was always going to be a strange atmosphere. Southampton had just gone into administration and while on the one hand that confirmed their relegation, it also meant that they could potentially avoid a ten point fine at the beginning of the following season by beating us.

I flew down to Southampton with my family, along with Barry and Sonya and a corporate finance friend called Tim Clarke, who had previously undertaken some advisory work for the club in the mid nineties when Dr Iven was a director. As I was reading my paper I overheard Tim say to Barry:

"Do you remember that meeting when Dr Iven said that we should talk to Colonel Gadaffi about raising some money?"

I couldn't quite believe my ears:

"What – are you joking?"

Apparently not. Colonel Gadaffi was keen to invest in the club in the nineties because when he grew up in the sixties Burnley was a big club and he had become a fan! I thought to myself, 'Can you imagine that – the BNP on the council and Colonel Gadaffi at the football club!' That's an eclectic mix for any town.

I'd never been to the St Marys Stadium before and we were hopeful that we would be celebrating by the end of the day. Even if we didn't win, we half expected to be through on the basis that Preston were unlikely to win at Birmingham. The Southampton boardroom was populated by accountants and administrators and I couldn't help but feel sorry for such a big club to be embroiled in such a mess. It's an impressive modern stadium and there were 25,000 fans at the match but they're bust and in the bottom three, all because of a series of bad decisions. Decisions at the top make or break football clubs.

We were lucky at half time to be only 2-1 down, but in the second half we were equally unlucky not to win it. It was a real battle and after the game ended in a 2-2 draw the Southampton fans gave us a good send off, invading the pitch and throwing whatever they had to hand at the Burnley fans.

We flew back and arrived in time to see the last ten minutes of the Preston game at the freight terminal in Manchester. It was 1-1 and so we got a bottle of champagne on ice to celebrate our likely achievement of reaching the play-offs. I spoke to Owen and he was boarding a plane to go up to Scotland to see some family. He said:

"Well it looks like Preston are going to draw, so I'll speak to you later Brendan – we could be there."

As we gathered round the television to watch the last few minutes, Ross Wallace, the Preston midfielder, stepped up and smacked a twenty-five yard free kick into the net. We were all quietly gutted and I thought, 'here we go again, bloody Preston are going to spoil the party for us.'

The initial reaction of despondency at the intensity of the moment was borne out of a real fear that Preston would indeed ruin it for us. But as the week wore on towards our last home game against Bristol City, we regained our composure and ambition. We had the Player of the Year Awards in the middle of the week and Barry and I were asked to speak. I went up first and Andy Hodgson, the host, asked me for a prediction for the match on Sunday against Bristol City. So I said:

"Without wishing to put a curse on the lads Andy, I think we'll win comfortably – 3-0."

Andy asked Barry the same question:

"Barry, do you think, like Brendan, that we'll win comfortably 3-0?"

And Barry replied:

"Oh no, no, no, no .....2-0!"

There was a genuine belief that we would beat Bristol and I left Owen to it. When there's a lot of tension before a match it's sensible to allow the manager and players the space to prepare. I did my best to relax Owen by sending my stock of funny jokes by text to lighten the moment. Owen didn't need anyone to tell him how much it meant to us all. He soaks up pressure well and I could see that his resolve was as strong as ever.

Early in the season I had organised a reunion for all the lads at Brunshaw Celtic for the final home game. We'd been mates since the early eighties and there were about thirty of us in a box in the James Hargreaves

Stand. We are all Burnley fans and it was a brilliant chance for me to share the occasion with the lads. The match itself was nervy to begin with, the ground was packed to the rafters and the players took a while to get into their stride. But after about half an hour Wade Elliott was dragged down to win a penalty, and when Graham Alexander duly stuck the ball in the net we all felt that one of our newly found heroes was going to lead us through to the play-offs. A couple of minutes later Wade scored with a sweet shot and Turf Moor erupted. I don't think Bristol City were really in the game after that. In the second half we played with freedom and ended up winning 4-0.

I had a night out with some of my old pals, wandering around Burnley and doing impromptu Q and As in the pubs as we passed through! We were all thrilled but when I spoke to Owen that night, although he was pleased, the over-riding sense was that he was filled with a desire to finish the job. As soon as we had reached the play-offs, Owen's objective was to get promoted and that's exactly where he was. In his words:

"We need get the last job done."

♦

Shortly after the Bristol City match I had a call from the secretary for the Chief Superintendant at Burnley police station, asking me if I could call in to see him that afternoon. So I went down to the Chief Super's office and we shared pleasantries for five minutes or so. I presumed that I was there because there must have been some serious hooligans that he wanted us to identify and isolate on match days, so I said:

"I was wondering what your reason was for asking me to call in."

The answer I got was not one I expected:

"Well Brendan, I wanted to say that over the past couple of years since the football club started to pick up,

things have been going better and better for us as well. The crime rate has dropped. Do you think you can keep it going that way?"

"*I'll have a go!*" I replied.

I hadn't foreseen a role in crime enforcement when I joined the board but it served to illustrate to me just what an impact the football club can have on our town. Shortly after, I met a local GP who told me that if Burnley won, there was hardly anyone in his waiting room on the following Monday morning. But if we lost his patients were queuing out of the door. So it seems that we were doing our bit for the Home Office and the Department of Health. I thought it best not to pass that extra burden onto Owen. He had recently been bestowed the title of 'God' by his rapidly growing hoards of adoring supporters. This recognition was first delivered by an American exiled Burnley fan with a good seat who held up his huge placard proclaiming, 'OWEN COYLE IS GOD' at a Wrestlemania event in the USA, getting some unexpected worldwide coverage for our manager. The proclamation spread through the streets of Burnley and Owen was formally adopted as our God!

♦

In the play-offs we all knew who we wanted to play and who we didn't want to play, although of course we didn't have the choice. We finished fifth so we were up against Reading, who were the pre-season favourites and probably the best football team in the division. But they'd had a shocking run of form, particularly at home, so we'd caught them at a good time. Their away form had been reasonably good so the biggest challenge was to beat them in the first leg at Turf Moor.

Straight after the Bristol match I rang Darren Bentley and chatted through our battle plan:

"*Look, we've got to start frightening the other clubs now. Let's put it out to the press that it's our destiny to be promoted this year. It's fifty years since we won the league and it's our destiny."*

All these incidental noises weigh on an opposing player's mind and if they keep reading that Burnley play attacking football, they've had big cup runs, it's their destiny and so on, it can all heighten the fear factor.

When the first leg of the play-off semi final arrived I was in York at the wedding of my niece, Rosemary. We had arranged to watch the second half of the match in a local pub and as soon as the speeches finished about ten of us jumped up and nipped round to the pub next door. In the pub there was a group of Burnley fans on a stag do and when I walked in they had a double take.

So we joined them and enjoyed the rest of the afternoon. The match itself had the look of a warm-up game for both sides. First leg play-offs are often like that but when we got a late penalty, Graham inevitably smashed it home and when Bikey was sent off and went into a frenzy that seemed to give us the psychological edge.

When we travelled down to Reading for the second leg I felt confident that we could do it. I genuinely thought we could win and apart from the first fifteen minutes during which Reading looked good, we took possession of the ball and I was still confident when we went in at half time 0-0. All Burnley fans will remember Martin Patterson's magnificent heart stopping thirty yard curler and our fans behind the goal erupted. But the second goal, Steve Thompson's cracker, was as momentous a goal to me as Jay Rod's against Spurs. When that went in we knew we had done it. We'd made it to Wembley and were one step away from satisfying the hunger that had been with the manager, players and fans ever since the cup semi-final. In truth, we won partly because we wanted it more. Reading is a middle England town. The club is sponsored by Waitrose and they had a team full of highly paid players who probably weren't hungry enough. We were sponsored by Hollands

Pies, and our philosophy is about hard working players with fighting spirit, togetherness and passion. We could beat anyone. And it was noticeable that at the end of the game, our players celebrated quietly and calmly. Graham Alexander was going round grabbing hold of the young lads and keeping their feet on the ground and there was an immediate controlled assurance in evidence. They contained their emotions brilliantly, and bottled up the adrenalin for the final. Alexander was outstanding. They must be going mad up in Preston!

The two goals in the second half at Reading will be permanently recorded in the memories of all Burnley fans. When the goal scorers, Patterson and Thompson, were interviewed by Sky after the match, the latter was asked:

"When you saw your goal fly in off that crossbar Steve, did you think in your heart of hearts it's job done?"

Thompson, struggling to contain his joy said:

"Well no, you don't like to... well Aye!" as he burst out laughing. We all felt that urge too. We were there, in the Play-Off Final. It was almost too good to be true. But it was true.

As we cracked a bottle of Waitrose Champagne in the boardroom, I saw John Madjedski having a conversation with Steve Coppell and overheard him say, 'all the best'. I thought that might be significant and later heard that Coppell had resigned.

In the car on the way home I received a call from Owen:

"How are we?" he ventured.

"Just a minute Owen" and then we all broke into a chorus of 'Da da da da da – Owen Coyle!' *"What do you think of that?"*

"The team did great," he said, *"I'm so pleased for you and the chairman."*

He never wavers from his dignity and humility and is always quick to dedicate our wins to the fans and the board. On the way home he sent me a text which read:

"Coppell's resigned" So I texted back:

"I thought he looked a bit more miserable than normal."

"He must be going on a world cruise on the salary he's on!" Owen replied.

At the end of the Reading game we had nothing to celebrate. We still had a job to finish. When I saw the Sheffield United Players jumping all over each other after they had beaten Preston in the other tie, I had a little smile to myself. And it hadn't gone unnoticed by Owen either. We were delighted of course but we were all part of a team that had to get over the final hurdle. The best contribution I could make was to help direct the PR. We continued the theme that it was our destiny and mixed it in with, 'we're the underdogs ..... and we have a never say die attitude.' Owen's great at this too, he'll take on any opportunity to go on TV and that helps the club. We're becoming an exciting club for players to come to and we're more of an achieving club now than a 'get by' club. Owen's total belief comes over and it's absolutely genuine. But he also believes that to do well in anything you have to be your own worst critic and he marries the two philosophies perfectly, reminiscent of the way Bill Shankly did.

Owen has already proved that he has the energy to go on and do great things and he can achieve more with less money than almost any manager in history that I can think of. But with the play-off final over a week away we all knew that we could only measure ourselves by what we had just achieved. We enjoyed the success but knew that was yesterday. Now we had just one final job to do.

14

Dare to Dream

May 25th 2009

'What separates the talented individual from the successful one is a lot of hard work.' Stephen King

It's only when you read it in the papers that it actually begins to sink in. We were all absolutely thrilled to be on the way to Wembley but there was still an air of bewilderment around the club. For Burnley fans, we've all had 33 years of waiting to get this far and to recognise that it's true, you sometimes need other people to tell you first. And I was no different to anyone else in that respect.

At board level, as you would expect, everyone was eagerly working out the consequences of us being in the final and what those would be if we actually won. But within our closed ranks Owen, Barry and I weren't counting any chickens. We were happy to be there but we understood that the job wasn't finished until we won the match. I didn't speak to Owen much until the last couple of days before the final. He wanted to have as much time with the players as possible and make sure that the bond of togetherness had become unbreakable. I carried on bombarding him with pathetic jokes in an attempt to keep his spirits high. And in the meantime I had met with his pal Alan Nixon, the Daily Mirror journalist, who had asked to do a piece on me before the final.

We talked about my early recollections of watching Burnley and the hopes we had of returning to the great days. Then he asked me about the Bad Beat Bob underpants incident at Chelsea before we moved on to talking about Owen. I actually told Alan that when we appointed Owen I didn't know him from Adam but that he reminded me a lot of Bill Shankly. When the article came out he had also featured Robbie's underpants and so the Mirror ran the creative headline, 'ADAM AND THE PANTS!'

As the big day approached we started to get more focussed and into match mindset and I sent a message that read:

"To get the win you, Sandy, Steve, Phil, the players, Barry, me and all the back up team have got to want it more than anything- for each other and for those close to us. That's what makes great clubs great."

Owen replied:

"I know we all do and Monday can't come quick enough."

I still wanted the smiles to flow so the day before the match I sent Owen another one which read:

"I've just had a call from a producer in Hollywood and George Clooney wants to star as you in the remake of 'A Shot at Glory'!"

Owen replied:

"That doesn't surprise me!"

The last text I sent to Owen was an omen from my Dad. The Guardian had run a piece saying that Burnley have played Sheffield United four times on the 25th of the month and won all four with twelve goals for and one goal against. Owen liked that!

♦

In the week before the play-off final I was coming under more and more pressure in my development business. The Wakefield development had stopped when Anglo Irish Bank called for a further fifty million pounds which we were unable to deliver. And I had a working capital facility with HBOS who, as a distressed bank, were very negative towards the whole property customer base and I was struggling.

Knowing that the tension was building up with HBOS I had been in discussions to bring in a new partner with fresh capital.   On the Wednesday I flew out to La Manga to meet with Kevin McCabe, the Sheffield United chairman, who, along with another party was interested in a new joint venture of my development business. Kevin and I have known each other for years. While our team had been to Portugal, the Sheffield lads had gone to La Manga and their team had flown back to Yorkshire the day before. A lot of the Sheffield staff were still there and I met up with Kevin and his group for dinner, the subject of the final came up often but it was all good humoured banter. As we went in for dinner I said to Kevin:

"Imagine if anyone from the press was here and saw us together."

At which point the first person he introduced me to was a chap called Tom from the BBC. I thought he was joking but as I sat next to Tom at dinner, he confirmed that he was indeed BBC Yorkshire's news presenter! We had a fairly limited conversation as you might expect.

♦

The day before the game, at nine in the morning, Ellen's Mum died. Her Mum had been poorly for several months and Ellen was considering not coming to the game because obviously she was very upset and she'd been up all the Saturday night with her Mum. I said to Ellen:

"If you don't feel up to it don't come. But if we win, it could be one of the most important days of my life and you won't be there."

And as destiny dictated, Ellen was with me.

It was a highly emotional time for us all, Ellen had lost her father in February and my Mum had died the July last year. Before we set off for Wembley I showed my Dad a picture that I had taken at our house just before Mum died and told him that I'd have it in my pocket on the day of the game. So if we did win it was for my Mum. Dad was deeply moved to think that would be the case and, of course, he felt just the same. We both hoped Mum would be there, cheering for us up in heaven.

We travelled down to London quite late on the Sunday with family and friends to the Stafford Hotel where we'd booked our accommodation. Ellen and I were both in a strange place. We'd lost three parents in the last twelve months. It had been a dreadful year for family and work but thankfully not for the football. We hoped that maybe with the weight of our representation 'up there' we might get something at Wembley.

◆

I had asked Stuart, the manager at the Stafford Hotel, who incidentally is a Blackburn fan (no matter), to line us up with a party in the hotel if we did win. There's a famous cellar there that's opened up for special events, Prince Charles had his stag do there and the England Cricket team celebrated the Ashes victory there in 2005. But we didn't want to officially book anything until we knew the result. So I asked Stuart to prepare something special if we did it.

The Stafford's clearly a very formal hotel and the dress code in the bar is blazers for gentlemen. We had planned to meet in the bar at nine, but abandoned that plan and hastily rearranged a get together in our room. We'd brought with us a few bottles of champagne, in the hope of a celebration, so we had a few drinks all crammed in our bedroom. Everybody was eager for the next day to come quickly.

Barry and Chris Duckworth were staying in the same hotel and I'd tried to meet them for a drink. When I went down to the bar later on there was just Chris and Liz Duckworth with two other couples who were Burnley fans. So we had a few more drinks and I shared my thoughts with Chris, who probably deserved and wanted the victory as much as anyone I know. Chris has had his own ups and downs but his passion for Burnley is phenomenal. He has two lovely sons and they're a fanatical family.

The next morning we grabbed breakfast and set off up to Wembley. We'd organised a few taxis to pick us up and it was bumper to bumper all the way to the ground, so it took over an hour to get there. Paul Fletcher had organised a tour to go round the stadium with a contact that he had at Wembley. I was able to take my group down onto the pitch. It was very humid and I hoped that our stamina was going to be as strong as it had been all season. We visited the dressing rooms and took some photographs there. My youngest son, Conor, was fascinated by the number of boots that Chris Eagles had, of many different colours. Clark Carlisle's pile of boots was about two feet deep as well! I wonder what our heroes of bygone days, like Jimmy McIlroy and Ralph Coates would think of that.

We then went back up to the Royal box which suffered from a power cut when we arrived. It was fairly hot in there for a while and all the time I was trying to hand over tickets for pals who were meeting me there. I was up and down the Wembley stairs like a yoyo and by the time we sat down for dinner I felt like I'd done a day's work. No sooner had I sat down than I was asked by a Wembley official if I could go and sign on behalf of the club for the drugs testing. So off I went back downstairs again to sign a form. Eventually I got back to the table, and just as I arrived Terry Robinson, the chief executive of Sheffield United, came over to speak to one of my guests, David Bartlett. After they'd had a quick chat, Dave leaned over to me and said:

"They're not happy.

"Why?" I asked.

"I'm not sure but when I asked him if they were ready for it he didn't seem confident at all."

There seemed to be less self belief within the Sheffield ranks which contrasted strongly with the expectation in our camp that this could be our day.

I'd organised for Conor and my godson, Joseph Tattersall, to be mascots, so before the match my good friend Steve Tattersall went down to the pitch with them. When the players came out it was brilliant to see Conor walking out with Steve Caldwell at the front of the team. He was thrilled with that and he'd been practising a few moves the week before!

For my part I was struggling to talk as I was trying my best to take it all in. To see the Clarets walking out on to the Wembley Turf and to see the mass of 37,000 Burnley fans, a waving sea of Claret and Blue, was the culmination of everything that Owen and the team had worked so hard for. This had to be our day. We might not get the chance again. I tried to watch what the players were doing and then I spotted Owen just pointing to his cheek as the camera was looking at him in the line up. He told me later that he was making sure they got his best side!

I probably wasn't the best person to sit next to because I was fully focussed on the game and not particularly talkative. For the first time I felt nervous and, as the match kicked off, in the opening ten minutes the team looked a little edgy as well. And then the unbelievable yet almost inevitable happened. Wade picked the ball up in the middle of the pitch and went on one of his mazy, speedy runs leaving two Sheffield players behind. He got the ball to Chris McCann on the edge of the box and then as the ball bounced back out to him from about twenty five yards he unleashed a swinging shot that flew into the top left corner of the net. Paddy Kenny in the Sheffield goal was nowhere near it. It was pandemonium. I know where the term 'over the moon' comes from now, as I was up there somewhere with Apollo Eleven. We'd scored! Half of the Stadium erupted and the explosion carried on for a good five minutes. Everyone in our box went mad, jumping around and Barry and Sonya nearly went over the balcony. But noticeably, on the pitch, the players weren't over celebrating, they were calming each other down and when I watched it replayed later I saw that Wade had a look of powerful, assured determination in his eyes that epitomised our team. I didn't feel that Sheffield would come back, and as the match wore on the chances we had for Robbie Blake and Joey Gudjonsson made me think that we would finish them off sooner rather than later. But Sheffield were defending magnificently and with the score at 1-0 there is always a nagging worry.

As the final whistle approached Ellen and I, along with thousands of other Clarets were almost praying for the final whistle. I touched my Mum's photo in my pocket and then it happened.

The final whistle went and there was bedlam. I've never heard a noise like it. Fans were on their phones to loved ones with not a hope in hell of hearing a word. We'd done it! We'd bloody well done it! I'd managed to get myself a pass to go down onto the pitch if we won. I had promised myself that if we were ever in that position I'd be on the pitch at full time. I wasn't bothered about being up in the Royal Box when we received the trophy. I wanted to be down on the pitch with Owen, Sandy and Steve and all the lads who'd made it happen. So I took off down the stairs and ran out onto the pitch to grab Owen, give him a big hug and say thanks. Then the next thing I knew Darren Bentley ran over and jumped on top of me and as the players were all celebrating on the pitch he pointed to the crowd and shouted:

"Look at this, look at this. We've done it!"

In the midst of the celebrations, as Owen and I walked over to the Coca Cola celebration platform behind the players holding up the trophy, Owen still had the presence of mind to say:

"Brendan, I was really sorry to hear about the death of Ellen's mother. You'll tell her I was asking won't you?"

And with that we were sprayed with champagne and tears of happiness. But that meant a lot to me.

Later, as the players walked passed us towards the steps Chris Eagles was crying with joy and Michael Duff jokingly said to me:

"I need to see you in three weeks time!" –hinting at a new contract.

I smiled and I thought, 'Oh oh, here we go.' I was delighted to have that problem of course.

Then I walked around the pitch to try to have a word with every player just to say thanks. I particularly wanted to tell the unsung heroes how much we thought about them, guys like Christian Kalvenes, who'd made such a difference to our defence. I caught Graham Alexander just after he'd been interviewed by Sky and seeing the youthful excitement in him, having won at Wembley, was outstanding. I said to him:

"Thank God we signed you from Preston."

Graham's presence in this team had given us another level and I could see that he was absolutely thrilled. And I can vividly remember Stephen Jordan drenched from top to toe in champagne hugging me as I thought, 'this suit is going to have to go to the dry cleaners!' Even the players who weren't involved were ecstatic. Alan Mahon said that he wished he'd achieved more at the club. There was a great team spirit and he'd never worked with a better manager than Owen. It was a privilege for me to be on the pitch with the players, looking at 37,000 fans cheering and singing and waving flags that read 'Owen Coyle is God'. I couldn't really pick anybody out in the crowd but I did manage to spot Alastair Campbell, who's about seven foot tall! And when I look back I wished I'd tried to kick a ball into the net but in all the excitement I forgot.

In amongst all the mayhem Owen seemed to be taking it all in his stride. Barry and I had a man hug and we shared a huge sense of joy and relief.

Ellen joined me on the pitch and later we went outside to meet the rest of our group and had a big family sing song. There were about thirty of us together, all Clarets and all scarcely believing our reality. Then I went back upstairs to try to make sure I'd shared the moment with everyone who'd played a part. Paul Fletcher was shedding a tear and we were thrilled for each other. And I thanked Gary Mellor because he'd been influential in helping us to get Martin Paterson in and to keep Wade. Gary had given us a lot of good advice and support and it would have been harder without him.

My phone was going like a parking meter and I had hundreds of emails and messages, one of which was from Phil Gartside, the Bolton chairman who was there at Wembley. I wanted to thank him for the part he played in referencing Owen but I didn't catch him. Then bizarrely as I walked out of the ground, who did I see in the traffic jam but Phil Gartside? As he opened the door and I leaned in to have a chat, I noticed there was almost a look of disbelief in his eyes. Burnley are actually in the Premiership.

"Hiya Phil, there's only one team in Lancashire now!"

♦

When we got back to the hotel, Stuart, the Blackburn fan, had lined up a brilliant do with red carpets, a big plasma screen showing the match, lots of photographs on the walls of the match highlights and a fabulous buffet. There were probably about eighty people back at the Stafford, comprising the directors and their families and guests and lots of different people associated with the club. Owen's mate Alan Nixon turned up and Tony Livesey joined us for a few drinks before he departed for Rome to commentate for the BBC on the Champions League final.

But one or two of the directors had barely shared the enjoyment of winning before they started worrying about the rumour of Celtic being after Owen. A group of us were determined to enjoy ourselves because I knew that wouldn't be the first thing on Owen's mind. I spoke to Owen a couple of times. He was at the Grosvenor with his family and the players and we agreed to meet the day after for the bus tour around the town.

But then at about half twelve that night while the Claret revellers were singing a chorus of 'Que Sera Sera', I had a phone call from Owen and I said:

"How are we Owen?"

"Wonderful Brendan, but I want to let you know that you might get a call from up the road?

"Up the road?" I said, but I knew what he meant. Celtic really did want him!

So I told him to try to enjoy what he'd achieved and any discussions we were going to have with anybody, just to put them out of his mind for a couple of days. He thanked me and suggested we meet up the following day for half an hour to catch up.

The morning after we took the train back up to Manchester and after a quick wash and brush up I headed off to Turf Moor for the bus tour and the staff party in the evening. Before the tour I met with Owen, and at that stage he didn't appear to be particularly interested in the possibility of an approach from Celtic. Neither Barry nor I had received any official contact from Glasgow so the three of us sat down for half an hour to have a general chat.

It was pandemonium on the top of the bus. As well as the team, all the directors were there and Radio Lancashire and Sky Sports were trying to do interviews. You could see the great camaraderie among the players and to see over 30,000 people on the streets in a sea of claret illustrated just what this all meant to our community. I thought about the comments that the Police Super had made and I could see that it was all worth while. Whatever angst and pressure we suffered in trying to get there it was clear that the club's achievement had made a difference to a lot of people's lives, and that was a tribute to everyone involved. Clark Carlisle and Steve Caldwell both told me that this meant a lot more to them than their respective achievements at Watford and Sunderland. In the past they had both expected to be promoted but here at Burnley it was an unbelievable moment. It is so obvious that the squad enjoy being together and the team spirit is unbeatable. I came away from that evening with the feeling that we had to try to avoid spoiling that next season at all costs. You can listen to the media pressure about buying players and spending money. But that might be foolhardy if you actually have a contented and gifted squad at your club already. We may need more squad depth to stay up but it's a delicate balance.

From a business viewpoint you have to consider why some teams do well and some teams don't do well in the Premier League, you have to look at the statistics. One of the reasons for failure might be that you don't invest enough money, but the main success factor is having the right type of people. The common denominator when we are selecting players is that we talk about bringing in the right type of player and if he's suitable for Burnley, and that's as much about his character as his footballing ability. Being in close proximity with the squad I felt that we had something special.

And these lads had changed the image of the town overnight. A few weeks ago if you googled Burnley you might bring up the BNP or some crime statistics. But now it's a Premier League town. And from an investment point of view the Premier League is commercially one of the most attractive products in the world. People don't necessarily see the cobbled streets any more, and our older fans no longer need to pull their hair out explaining that we used to be in the top division. From my point of view we had done what I had hoped we'd do which was to progress every year. When I joined the board the target I gave myself was to help the club to get to the Premiership within five years and be established there within ten. While you need a bit of luck and you need your decisions to come good I felt that a lot of hard work was being rewarded. But now becoming established in the Premiership is the new objective and at that moment keeping Owen at the club was essential. The chemistry and shared ethos between owners and manager needs to be right and we knew that we'd struggle to replace Owen. So the next day Barry, Owen and I got together and, after sharing our thoughts on the future, agreed he was staying and we could look forward to next season.

Later that day I had a call from Radio Lancashire saying that they believed Owen Coyle was going to be signing for Celtic that afternoon. So I said:

"I am one hundred per cent certain that Owen Coyle will be our manager at the start of next season."

Just as I put the phone down one of my guys in the office, who is a Celtic fan walked in and said:

"Bren, some guy has just gone into the bookies in Glasgow in front of my mate and put ten grand on Owen Coyle to be the next Celtic manager!"

And I thought, 'Shit.' I later rang Owen, and we quickly laughed it off. But from that Wednesday speculation was running wild in the town and it almost reached a level of hysteria among Burnley fans who were taunting themselves by reading inflammatory commentary in the Scottish press. The Clarets Mad website was engulfed by numerous threads and comments by people who knew Owen was going or knew he was staying. One contributor noted that at teatime on Wednesday, significantly all the Burnley Directors had just arrived at Turf Moor. But in truth that was just for a scheduled board meeting. I wasn't there and Owen was already packing for his holidays.

A few weeks later we were able to announce Owen's new four year contract and Burnley's chosen God was here to stay.

♦

That glorious week ended dreadfully for me as HBOS, for their own reasons, decided to appoint an administrator to my development business. It really hurt me and my senior management team but we have battled on since to restart that division of the group. The juxtaposition of experiences could not be more extreme. But several days later my brother Chris's wife, Catherine, died suddenly. As a family we were grief stricken and it certainly gave me a perspective on how fortunate I have been in most respects.

♦

There are some things that have to happen quickly for the coming season. While the town bit its nails at the prospect of Celtic prizing Owen away rumours started to flow about who we might be signing, from the sublime to the ridiculous. I have shared a business interest with Gary Neville and Ryan Giggs for over a year now, and during the ten days after the play –off final I had arranged to go to Dubai with Ryan Giggs. While we were in the departure lounge I decided to buy some magazines and Ryan said he'd come with me. We must have stopped a dozen times on the way to and from WH

Smiths for him to sign autographs and I jokingly said to him:

"It's just the same for me back in Burnley you know!"

An hour later as we got settled in our seats on the plane, I noticed a guy boarding who was wearing a Burnley shirt. He looked at Ryan and then looked over to me and in a gasp of wonder said:

"Brendan?"

I leaned over to Ryan and said:

"See what I mean?!"

So ever quick to sniff out a story, the Clarets Mad message board announced the sighting and within a few hours wild speculation spread of Ryan potentially being a transfer target.

During my visits to the Middle East, as I am associated with Burnley, businessmen always want to speak to me about football. The Premier League is such an alluring package globally. But it's always great to talk about football for any football fan. And I'm no different to most fans.

One evening I was asked to meet the King of Bahrain's right hand man, a chap called Fahad, who was interested in Modus projects. So I agreed to meet him and he brought along a gentleman he referred to as 'Prince'. We discussed business generally but it soon became evident that 'Prince' had a keen interest in Premier League football as well and he wanted to talk about Burnley, so we chatted generally about the club.

Later we were unexpectedly joined by the Nigerian prime minister's chief advisor. He was educated at Harrow and I learnt that all the major Nigerian corporate transactions are managed by him. I enjoyed the meeting and recognised that I was in the esteemed company of the King of Bahrain's right hand man, Nigeria's 'Mr Fixit' and a guy called 'Prince'. After a couple of hours I had to go to another function so I made my apologies and left. As I got in the lift I was followed in by Mr Fixit and we chatted about follow up discussions regarding potential investment in a new project in the Middle East. I took the opportunity of asking him whether 'Prince' had any money, and he answered:

"Are you kidding me?"

"No why, who is he?"

"He's Colonel Gadaffi's son!"

Oh no! I couldn't believe it. It seems like the Gadaffi family are still keen to become Burnley fans but I hadn't left my number.

◆

We've already made some exciting player signings this summer. We'd been working on the move for David Edgar since I met his agent out in America in February. And Tyrone Mears and Steven Fletcher are both Premiership quality players. They all fit our model of talented, quick, young and, most of all, desperately hungry young players who want to make a name for themselves. But the best signing of the summer by a mile is the hungriest of them all. What Owen has achieved in the short time he has been with us has exceeded all our expectations. And no one was trying to offend the ecclesiastical sector when they made their 'Owen Coyle is God' banners in readiness for the most memorable day in thousands of Clarets fans lives.

Owen has been called a few things in his time. He's called himself George Clooney and when we appointed him back in 2007 I called him the new Bill Shankly. He's from Glasgow, a teetotaller and he has the same steely determination as the great man. With his unique attitude to life and football I believe that Owen is destined to become a great manager. When we first spoke I was struck by his honesty and dignity, and Alex McLeish was entirely correct in his reference for Owen by predicting that he would become a Premier League manager one day.

Well that day has come rather sooner than some people expected, in fact within two years of his appointment. Owen's latest win to game ratio is 48% - and Bill Shankly's was 50%!

♦

So there you have it. Two and a half years in the sometimes wonderful world of football and the precarious but thrilling world of property and finance. I didn't follow a well trodden path. I did my own thing and while I haven't been able to please everyone, I have been part of the rollercoaster ride where Burnley has become everyone's 'favourite other team' all around the world.

Sometimes you don't need armies of advisors, you just need a small collection of dedicated people who Dare to Dream.

Barry Kilby – Chairman of Burnley Football Club 1998 – Present Day

In sharing my memories of the last two and a half years as a director of Burnley Football Club, I want to pay tribute to the man who helped to lay the foundations on which a new era for our great club is being built.

Barry assumed the stewardship as Chairman at Turf Moor over ten years ago, and so took the responsibility to inspire a period of progress that brought renewed pride and hope to thousands of Clarets. We recognised his value when, in his first full season at the helm, Burnley were promoted in 2000.

To lead a football club, which in itself represents a difficult business model, into the Championship is a courageous commitment for anyone.

Barry is a local lad and can recount stories of matches in black and white days! And he evidenced his own playing prowess, turning out for our reserves one season. He loves football generally, which you need on the board to prop up enthusiasm when things aren't perhaps working out as planned.

I first met Barry when he and Ray Ingleby came to see me to invite further investment to the club. We have since enjoyed each others company and a good working relationship: hence the 'team approach' where we act together as operational directors.

The events of May 25th this year at Wembley have fulfilled Barry and his wife Sonya's dreams, and there can be no greater thrill for a fan than to lead his club into the promised land of the Premiership.

I have thoroughly enjoyed working with Barry since joining the board and our trip to the US in the summer of 2008 brought us closer together as friends, and I noticed a real excitement returning for Barry and his hopes for the club, after suffering the shock of near administration following the collapse of ITV Digital. This year has brought some unforgettable football moments, but off the pitch we have had to pedal fast to keep this wonderful team together.

I have been grateful for the whole experience and the future now looks fascinating and I hope one day soon that our sustained success will enable Barry to resoundingly say *'Katy bar the door'*, as we work to make the club strong for the next generation of Clarets.

Brendan

The phrase 'Katy Bar the door', often used by Barry is taken from James Riley's poem *'When Lide Married Him' (1894)* – and means 'as long as we're all inside, we're safe!'

Burnley F.C. Promotion Winning Team 2008/2009

Manager: Owen Coyle

Assistant Manager: Sandy Stewart

First Team Coach: Steve Davis

Goalkeeping Coach: Phil Hughes

Players: Brian Jensen, Diego Penny, Rhys Williams, Graham Alexander, Christian Kalvenes, Michael Duff, Clark Carlisle, Steven Caldwell (Captain), Kevin McDonald, Joey Gudjonsson, Ade Akinbiyi, Martin Paterson, Wade Elliot, Steve Jones, Chris McCann, Gabor Kiraly, Alan Mahon, Jay Rodriguez, Robbie Blake, Besart Berisha, Stephen Jordan, Russell Anderson, Adam Kay, Remco Van Der Schaaf, Alex MacDonald, Steven Thompson, Chris Eagles.

Directors: Barry Kilby, Brendan Flood, Ray Ingleby, Clive Holt, John Turkington, Chris Duckworth, Martin Hobbs, John Sullivan, Ray Griffiths, Mike Garlick.

Chief Executive: Paul Fletcher MBE

Club Secretary: Pauline Scott

Chief Scout: Cliff Roberts

Head Physiotherapist: Andy Mitchell

Director of Youth Development: Martin Dobson

Centre of Excellence Manager: Vince Overson

Youth Team Coach: Terry Pashley

Head of Recruitment: Jeff Taylor

Education and Welfare Officer: Pat McKiernon

Medical Officers: Dr M. McDevitt, Dr I Maudsley

Ground Safety Officer: Alex Wood

Stadium Manager: Doug Metcalf

Financial Controller: Ken Stout

Catering Manager: Chris Gibson

Director of Commercial Affairs: Anthony Fairclough

Media Manager: Darren Bentley

Marketing Executive: Nick Taylor

Retail Manager: Paul Stanworth

Ticket Office Manager: Elaine Clare

Club Historian: Ray Simpson

Head of Community Sports Trust: Louise Spencer

.... and the 37,000 supporters at Wembley